DEPARTMENT OF THE NAVY
HEADQUARTERS UNITED STATES MARINE CORPS
3000 MARINE CORPS PENTAGON
WASHINGTON, D.C. 20350-3000

I0426118

MUSIC TRAINING AND READINESS MANUAL

DEPARTMENT OF THE NAVY
HEADQUARTERS UNITED STATES MARINE CORPS
3000 MARINE CORPS PENTAGON
WASHINGTON, D.C. 20350-3000

NAVMC 3500.28A
C 469
15 Feb 2011

NAVMC 3500.28A

From: Commandant of the Marine Corps
To: Distribution List

Subj: MUSIC TRAINING AND READINESS MANUAL, (SHORT TITLE: MUSIC T&R MANUAL)

Ref: (a) MCO P3500.72A
      (b) MCO 1553.3A
      (c) MCO 3400.3F
      (d) MCO 3500.27B W/Erratum
      (e) MCRP 3-0A
      (f) MCRP 3-0B
      (g) MCO 1553.2A

1. <u>Purpose</u>. Per reference (a), this T&R Manual establishes Core Capability Mission Essential Tasks (MET) for readiness reporting and required events for standardization training of Marine personnel assigned to perform Marine Corps Occupational Field 55/Music functions. Additionally, it provides tasking for formal schools preparing personnel for service in the Marine Corps Music field. This NAVMC supersedes NAVMC 3500.28.

2. <u>Scope</u>

   a. The Core Capability Mission Essential Task List (METL) in this manual is used in Defense Readiness Reporting System (DRRS) for the assessment and reporting of unit readiness. Units achieve training readiness for reporting in DRRS by gaining and sustaining proficiency in the training events in this manual at both collective (unit) and individual levels.

   b. Per reference (b), commanders will conduct an internal assessment of the unit's ability to execute each MET, and develop long-, mid-, and short-range training plans to sustain proficiency in each MET. Training plans will incorporate these events to standardize training and provide objective assessment of progress toward attaining combat readiness. Commanders will keep records at the unit and individual levels to record training achievements, identify training gaps, and document objective assessments of readiness associated with training Marines. Commanders will use reference (c) to incorporate nuclear, biological, and chemical defense training into training plans and reference (d) to integrate operational risk management. References (e) and (f) provide amplifying information for effective planning and management of training within the unit.

   c. Formal school and training detachment commanders will use references (a) and (g) to ensure programs of instruction meet skill training requirements established in this manual, and provide career-progression

DISTRIBUTION STATEMENT A: Approved for public release; distribution is unlimited.

training in the events designated for initial training in the formal school environment.

4. <u>Information</u>. CG, TECOM will update this T&R Manual as necessary to provide current and relevant training standards to commanders, and to ensure a current Core Capabilities METL is available for use in DRRS. All questions pertaining to the Marine Corps Ground T&R Program and Unit Training Management should be directed to: Commanding General, TECOM (Ground Training Division C 469), 1019 Elliot Road, Quantico, VA 22134.

5. <u>Command</u>. This Directive is applicable to the Marine Corps Total Force.

6. <u>Certification</u>. Reviewed and approved this date.

R. C. FOX
By direction

Distribution: PCN 10033196500

    Copy to: 7000260 (2)
             8145001 (1)

LOCATOR SHEET

Subj: MUSIC TRAINING AND READINESS MANUAL, (SHORT TITLE: MUSIC T&R MANUAL)

Location: _____
              (Indicate location(s) of copy(ies) of this Manual.)

RECORD OF CHANGES

Log completed change action as indicated.

Change Number	Date of Change	Date Entered	Signature of Person Incorporated Change

MUSIC T&R MANUAL

TABLE OF CONTENTS

CHAPTER 1

OVERVIEW

MUSIC T&R MANUAL

CHAPTER 1

OVERVIEW

1000. INTRODUCTION

1. The T&R Program is the Corps' primary tool for planning, conducting and evaluating training and assessing training readiness. Subject Matter Experts (SMEs) from the operating forces developed core capability Mission Essential Task Lists (METLs) for ground communities derived from the Marine Corps Task List (MCTL). T&R Manuals are built around these METLs and all events contained in T&R Manuals relate directly to this METL. This comprehensive T&R Program will help to ensure the Marine Corps continues to improve its combat readiness by training more efficiently and effectively. Ultimately, this will enhance the Marine Corps' ability to accomplish real-world missions.

2. The T&R Manual contains the individual and collective training requirements to prepare units to accomplish their combat mission. The T&R Manual is not intended to be an encyclopedia that contains every minute detail of how to accomplish training. Instead, it identifies the minimum standards that Marines must be able to perform in combat. The T&R Manual is a fundamental tool for commanders to build and maintain unit combat readiness. Using this tool, leaders can construct and execute an effective training plan that supports the unit's METL. More detailed information on the Marine Corps Ground T&R Program is found in reference (a).

1001. UNIT TRAINING

1. The training of Marines to perform as an integrated unit in combat lies at the heart of the T&R program. Unit and individual readiness are directly related. Individual training and the mastery of individual core skills serve as the building blocks for unit combat readiness. A Marine's ability to perform critical skills required in combat is essential. However, it is not necessary to have all individuals within a unit fully trained in order for that organization to accomplish its assigned tasks. Manpower shortfalls, temporary assignments, leave, or other factors outside the commander's control, often affect the ability to conduct individual training. During these periods, unit readiness is enhanced if emphasis is placed on the individual training of Marines on-hand. Subsequently, these Marines will be mission ready and capable of executing as part of a team when the full complement of personnel is available.

2. Commanders will ensure that all tactical training is focused on their combat mission. The T&R Manual is a tool to help develop the unit's training plan. In most cases, unit training should focus on achieving unit proficiency in the core capabilities METL. However, commanders will adjust their training focus to support METLs associated with a major OPLAN/CONPLAN or named operation as designated by their higher commander and reported accordingly in the Defense Readiness Reporting System (DRRS). Tactical

training will support the METL in use by the commander and be tailored to meet T&R standards. Commanders at all levels are responsible for effective combat training. The conduct of training in a professional manner consistent with Marine Corps standards cannot be over emphasized.

3. Commanders will provide personnel the opportunity to attend formal and operational level courses of instruction as required by this Manual. Attendance at all formal courses must enhance the warfighting capabilities of the unit as determined by the unit commander.

1002. UNIT TRAINING MANAGEMENT

1. Unit Training Management (UTM) is the application of the Systems Approach to Training (SAT) and the Marine Corps Training Principles. This is accomplished in a manner that maximizes training results and focuses the training priorities of the unit in preparation for the conduct of its wartime mission.

2. UTM techniques, described in references (b) and (e), provide commanders with the requisite tools and techniques to analyze, design, develop, implement, and evaluate the training of their unit. The Marine Corps Training Principles, explained in reference (b), provide sound and proven direction and are flexible enough to accommodate the demands of local conditions. These principles are not inclusive, nor do they guarantee success. They are guides that commanders can use to manage unit-training programs. The Marine Corps training principles are:

- Train as you fight
- Make commanders responsible for training
- Use standards-based training
- Use performance-oriented training
- Use mission-oriented training
- Train the MAGTF to fight as a combined arms team
- Train to sustain proficiency
- Train to challenge

3. To maintain an efficient and effective training program, leaders at every level must understand and implement UTM. Guidance for UTM and the process for establishing effective programs are contained in references (a) through (g).

1003. SUSTAINMENT AND EVALUATION OF TRAINING

1. The evaluation of training is necessary to properly prepare Marines for combat. Evaluations are either formal or informal, and performed by members of the unit (internal evaluation) or from an external command (external evaluation).

2. Marines are expected to maintain proficiency in the training events for their MOS at the appropriate grade or billet to which assigned. Leaders are responsible for recording the training achievements of their Marines. Whether it involves individual or collective training events, they must ensure proficiency is sustained by requiring retraining of each event at or

before expiration of the designated sustainment interval. Performance of the training event, however, is not sufficient to ensure combat readiness. Leaders at all levels must evaluate the performance of their Marines and the unit as they complete training events, and only record successful accomplishment of training based upon the evaluation. The goal of evaluation is to ensure that correct methods are employed to achieve the desired standard, or the Marines understand how they need to improve in order to attain the standard. Leaders must determine whether credit for completing a training event is recorded if the standard was not achieved. While successful accomplishment is desired, debriefing of errors can result in successful learning that will allow ethical recording of training event completion. Evaluation is a continuous process that is integral to training management and is conducted by leaders at every level and during all phases of planning and the conduct of training. To ensure training is efficient and effective, evaluation is an integral part of the training plan. Ultimately, leaders remain responsible for determining if the training was effective.

3. The purpose of formal and informal evaluation is to provide commanders with a process to determine a unit's/Marine's proficiency in the tasks that must be performed in combat. Informal evaluations are conducted during every training evolution. Formal evaluations are often scenario-based, focused on the unit's METs, based on collective training standards, and usually conducted during higher-level collective events. References (a) and (f) provide further guidance on the conduct of informal and formal evaluations using the Marine Corps Ground T&R Program.

1004. ORGANIZATION

1. T&R Manuals are organized in one of two methods: unit-based or community-based. Unit-based T&R Manuals are written to support a type of unit (Infantry, Artillery, Tanks, etc.) and contain both collective and individual training standards. Community-based are written to support an Occupational Field, a group of related Military Occupational Specialties (MOSs), or billets within an organization (EOD, NBC, Intel, etc.), and usually only contain individual training standards. T&R Manuals are comprised of chapters that contain unit METs, collective training standards (CTS), and individual training standards (ITS) for each MOS, billet, etc.

2. The Tank T&R Manual is a unit-based manual comprised of 10 chapters. Chapter 2 lists the Core Capability METs and their related Battalion and Company-level events. Chapters 3 through 8 contain collective events. Chapters 9 and 10 contain individual events.

1005. T&R EVENT CODING

1. T&R events are coded for ease of reference. Each event has up-to a 4-4-4-digit identifier. The first up-to four digits are referred to as a "community" and represent the unit type or occupation (TANK, TOW, 1802, etc.). The second up-to four digits represent the functional or duty area (TAC, CMDC, GNRY, etc.). The last four digits represent the level and sequence of the event.

2. The T&R levels are illustrated in Figure 1. An example of the T&R coding used in this Manual is shown in Figure 2.

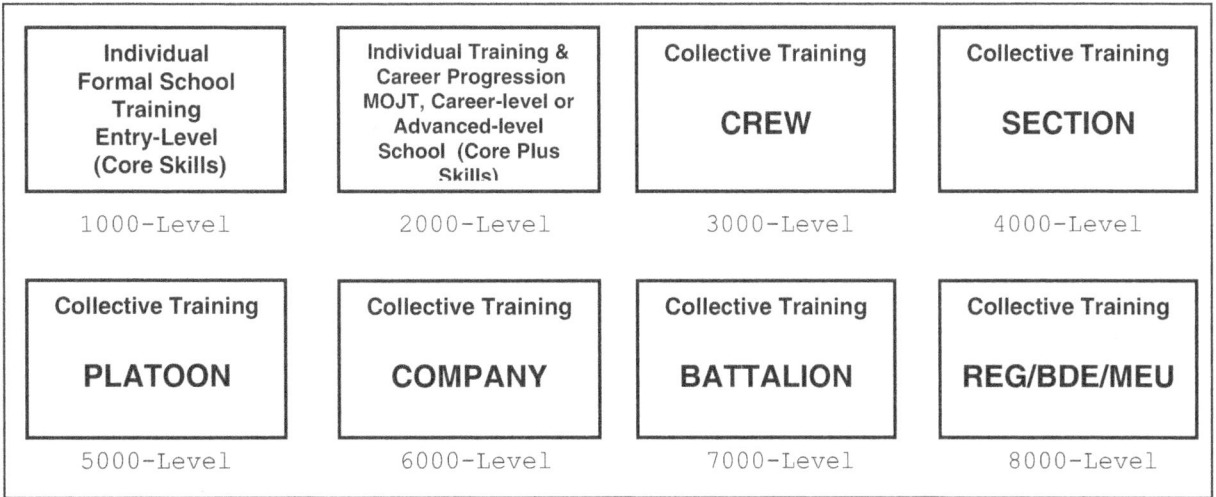

Figure 1: T&R Event Levels

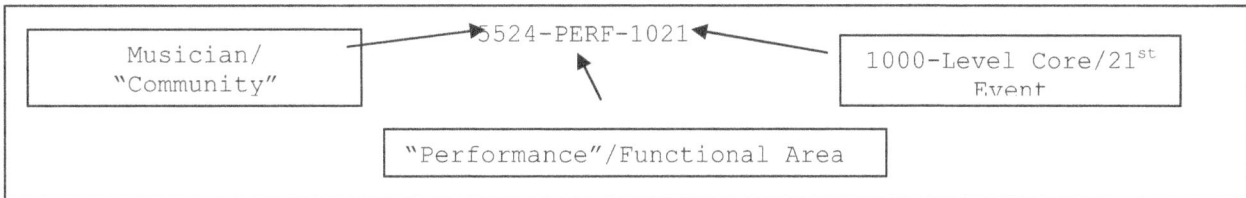

Figure 2: T&R Event Coding

1006. COMBAT READINESS PERCENTAGE

1. The Marine Corps Ground T&R Program includes processes to assess readiness of units and individual Marines. Every unit in the Marine Corps maintains a basic level of readiness based on the training and experience of the Marines in the unit. Even units that never trained together are capable of accomplishing some portion of their missions. Combat readiness assessment does not associate a quantitative value for this baseline of readiness, but uses a "Combat Readiness Percentage", as a method to provide a concise descriptor of the recent training accomplishments of units and Marines.

2. Combat Readiness Percentage (CRP) is the percentage of required training events that a unit or Marine accomplishes within specified sustainment intervals.

3. In unit-based T&R Manuals, unit combat readiness is assessed as a percentage of the successfully completed and current (within sustainment interval) key training events called "Evaluation-Coded" (E-Coded) Events. E-Coded Events and unit CRP calculation are described in follow-on paragraphs. CRP achieved through the completion of E-Coded Events is directly relevant to readiness assessment in DRRS.

4. Individual combat readiness, in both unit-based and community-based T&R Manuals, is assessed as the percentage of required individual events in which a Marine is current. This translates as the percentage of training events for his/her MOS and grade (or billet) that the Marine successfully completes within the directed sustainment interval. Individual skills are developed through a combination of 1000-level training (entry-level formal school courses), individual on-the-job training in 2000-level events, and follow-on formal school training. Skill proficiency is maintained by retraining in each event per the specified sustainment interval.

1007. EVALUATION-CODED (E-CODED) EVENTS

1. Unit-type T&R Manuals can contain numerous unit events, some for the whole unit and others for integral parts that serve as building blocks for training. To simplify training management and readiness assessment, only collective events that are critical components of a mission essential task (MET), or key indicators of a unit's readiness, are used to generate CRP for a MET. These critical or key events are designated in the T&R Manual as Evaluation-Coded (E-Coded) events. Formal evaluation of unit performance in these events is recommended because of their value in assessing combat readiness. Only E-Coded events are used to calculate CRP for each MET.

2. The use of a METL-based training program allows the commander discretion in training. This makes the T&R Manual a training tool rather than a prescriptive checklist.

1008. CRP CALCULATION

1. Collective training begins at the 3000 level (team, crew or equivalent). Unit training plans are designed to accomplish the events that support the unit METL while simultaneously sustaining proficiency in individual core skills. Using the battalion-based (unit) model, the battalion (7000-level) has collective events that directly support a MET on the METL. These collective events are E-Coded and the only events that contribute to unit CRP. This is done to assist commanders in prioritizing the training toward the METL, taking into account resource, time, and personnel constraints.

2. Unit CRP increases after the completion of E-Coded events. The number of E-Coded events for the MET determines the value of each E-Coded event. For example, if there are 4 E-Coded events for a MET, each is worth 25% of MET CRP. MET CRP is calculated by adding the percentage of each completed and current (within sustainment interval) E-Coded training event. The percentage for each MET is calculated the same way and all are added together and divided by the number of METS to determine unit CRP. For ease of calculation, we will say that each MET has 4 E-Coded events, each contributing 25% towards the completion of the MET. If the unit has completed and is current on three of the four E-Coded events for a given MET, then they have completed 75% of the MET. The CRP for each MET is added together and divided by the number of METS to get unit CRP; unit CRP is the average of MET CRP.

For Example:

```
MET 1:  75% complete  (3 of 4 E-Coded events trained)
MET 2:  100% complete (6 of 6 E-Coded events trained)
MET 3:  25% complete  (1 of 4 E-Coded events trained)
MET 4:  50% complete  (2 of 4 E-Coded events trained)
MET 5:  75% complete  (3 of 4 E-Coded events trained)
```

To get unit CRP, simply add the CRP for each MET and divide by the number of METS:

MET CRP: 75 + 100 + 25 + 50 + 75 = 325

Unit CRP: 325 (total MET CRP)/5 (total number of METS) = 65%

1009. T&R EVENT COMPOSITION

1. This section explains each of the components of a T&R event. These items are included in all events in each T&R Manual.

   a. Event Code (see Sect 1006). The event code is a 4-4-4 character set. For individual training events, the first 4 characters indicate the occupational function. The second 4 characters indicate functional area (TAC, CBTS, VOPS, etc.). The third 4 characters are simply a numerical designator for the event.

   b. Event Title. The event title is the name of the event.

   c. E-Coded. This is a "yes/no" category to indicate whether or not the event is E-Coded. If yes, the event contributes toward the CRP of the associated MET. The value of each E-Coded event is based on number of E-Coded events for that MET. Refer to paragraph 1008 for detailed explanation of E-Coded events.

   d. Supported MET(s). List all METs that are supported by the training event.

   e. Sustainment Interval. This is the period, expressed in number of months, between evaluation or retraining requirements. Skills and capabilities acquired through the accomplishment of training events are refreshed at pre-determined intervals. It is essential that these intervals are adhered to in order to ensure Marines maintain proficiency.

   f. Billet. Individual training events may contain a list of billets within the community that are responsible for performing that event. This ensures that the billet's expected tasks are clearly articulated and a Marine's readiness to perform in that billet is measured.

   g. Grade. Each individual training event will list the rank(s) at which Marines are required to learn and sustain the training event.

   h. Initial Training Setting. For Individual T&R Events only, this specifies the location for initial instruction of the training event in one of three categories (formal school, managed on-the-job training, distance learning). Regardless of the specified Initial Training Setting, any T&R event may be introduced and evaluated during managed on-the-job training.

       (1) "FORMAL" – When the Initial Training Setting of an event is identified as "FORMAL" (formal school), the appropriate formal school or training detachment is required to provide initial training in the event. Conversely, formal schools and training detachments are not authorized to provide training in events designated as Initial Training Setting "MOJT" or "DL." Since the duration of formal school training must be constrained to optimize Operating Forces' manning, this element provides the mechanism for Operating Forces' prioritization of training requirements for both entry-level (1000-level) and career-level (2000-level) T&R Events. For formal schools and training detachments, this element defines the requirements for content of courses.

       (2) "DL" – Identifies the training event as a candidate for initial training via a Distance Learning product (correspondence course or MarineNet course).

       (3) "MOJT" – Events specified for Managed On-the-Job Training are to be introduced to Marines, and evaluated, as part of training within a unit by supervisory personnel.

   i. Event Description. Provide a description of the event purpose, objectives, goals, and requirements. It is a general description of an action requiring learned skills and knowledge (e.g. Camouflage the M1A1 Tank).

   j. Condition. Describe the condition(s), under which tasks are performed. Conditions are based on a "real world" operational environment. They indicate what is provided (equipment, materials, manuals, aids, etc.), environmental constraints, conditions under which the task is performed, and any specific cues or indicators to which the performer must respond. When resources or safety requirements limit the conditions, this is stated.

   k. Standard. The standard indicates the basis for judging effectiveness of the performance. It consists of a carefully worded statement that identifies the proficiency level expected when the task is performed. The standard provides the minimum acceptable performance parameters and is strictly adhered to. The standard for collective events is general, describing the desired end-state or purpose of the event. While the standard for individual events specifically describe to what proficiency level in terms of accuracy, speed, sequencing, quality of performance, adherence to procedural guidelines, etc., the event is accomplished.

   l. Event Components. Describe the actions composing the event and help the user determine what must be accomplished and to properly plan for the event.

   m. Prerequisite Events. Prerequisites are academic training or other T&R events that must be completed prior to attempting the task. They are lower-level events or tasks that give the individual/unit the skills required to accomplish the event. They can also be planning steps, administrative requirements, or specific parameters that build toward mission accomplishment.

n. <u>Chained Events</u>. Collective T&R events are supported by lower-level collective and individual T&R events. This enables unit leaders to effectively identify subordinate T&R events that ultimately support specific mission essential tasks. When the accomplishment of any upper-level events, by their nature, result in the performance of certain subordinate and related events, the events are "chained." The completion of chained events will update sustainment interval credit (and CRP for E-Coded events) for the related subordinate level events.

o. <u>Related Events</u>. Provide a list of all Individual Training Standards that support the event.

p. <u>References</u>. The training references are utilized to determine task performance steps, grading criteria, and ensure standardization of training procedures. They assist the trainee in satisfying the performance standards, or the trainer in evaluating the effectiveness of task completion. References are also important to the development of detailed training plans.

q. <u>Distance Learning Products</u> (IMI, CBT, MCI, etc.). Include this component when the event can be taught via one of these media methods vice attending a formal course of instruction or receiving MOJT.

r. <u>Support Requirements</u>. This is a list of the external and internal support the unit and Marines will need to complete the event. The list includes, but is not limited to:

- Range(s)/Training Area
- Ordnance
- Equipment
- Materials
- Other Units/Personnel
- Other Support Requirements

s. <u>Miscellaneous</u>. Provide any additional information that assists in the planning and execution of the event. Miscellaneous information may include, but is not limited to:

- Admin Instructions
- Special Personnel Certifications
- Equipment Operating Hours
- Road Miles

2. Community-based T&R Manuals have several additional components not found in unit-based T&R Manuals. These additions do not apply to this T&R Manual.

1010. CBRNE TRAINING

1. All personnel assigned to the operating force must be trained in chemical, biological, radiological, nuclear, and explosive incident defense (CBRNE), in order to survive and continue their mission in this environment. Individual proficiency standards are defined as survival and basic operating standards. Survival standards are those that the individual must master in order to survive CBRNE attacks. Basic operating standards are those that the

individual, and collectively the unit, must perform to continue operations in a CBRNE environment.

2. In order to develop and maintain the ability to operate in an CBRNE environment, CBRNE training is an integral part of the training plan and events in this T&R Manual. Units should train under CBRNE conditions whenever possible. Per reference (c), all units must be capable of accomplishing their assigned mission in a contaminated environment.

1011. NIGHT TRAINING

1. While it is understood that all personnel and units of the operating force are capable of performing their assigned mission in "every climate and place," current doctrine emphasizes the requirement to perform assigned missions at night and during periods of limited visibility. Basic skills are significantly more difficult when visibility is limited.

2. To ensure units are capable of accomplishing their mission they must train under the conditions of limited visibility. Units should strive to conduct all events in this T&R Manual during both day and night/limited visibility conditions. When there is limited training time available, night training should take precedence over daylight training, contingent on individual, crew, and unit proficiency.

1012. OPERATIONAL RISK MANAGEMENT (ORM)

1. ORM is a process that enables commanders to plan for and minimize risk while still accomplishing the mission. It is a decision making tool used by Marines at all levels to increase operational effectiveness by anticipating hazards and reducing the potential for loss, thereby increasing the probability of a successful mission. ORM minimizes risks to acceptable levels, commensurate with mission accomplishment.

2. Commanders, leaders, maintainers, planners, and schedulers will integrate risk assessment in the decision-making process and implement hazard controls to reduce risk to acceptable levels. Applying the ORM process will reduce mishaps, lower costs, and provide for more efficient use of resources. ORM assists the commander in conserving lives and resources and avoiding unnecessary risk, making an informed decision to implement a course of action (COA), identifying feasible and effective control measures where specific measures do not exist, and providing reasonable alternatives for mission accomplishment. Most importantly, ORM assists the commander in determining the balance between training realism and unnecessary risks in training, the impact of training operations on the environment, and the adjustment of training plans to fit the level of proficiency and experience of Sailors/Marines and leaders. Further guidance for ORM is found in references (b) and (d).

1013. APPLICATION OF SIMULATION

1. Simulations/Simulators and other training devices shall be used when they are capable of effectively and economically supplementing training on the

identified training task. Particular emphasis shall be placed on simulators that provide training that might be limited by safety considerations or constraints on training space, time, or other resources. When deciding on simulation issues, the primary consideration shall be improving the quality of training and consequently the state of readiness. Potential savings in operating and support costs normally shall be an important secondary consideration.

2. Each training event contains information relating to the applicability of simulation. If simulator training applies to the event, then the applicable simulator(s) is/are listed in the "Simulation" section and the CRP for simulation training is given. This simulation training can either be used in place of live training, at the reduced CRP indicated; or can be used as a precursor training for the live event, i.e., weapons simulators, convoy trainers, observed fire trainers, etc. It is recommended that tasks be performed by simulation prior to being performed in a live-fire environment. However, in the case where simulation is used as a precursor for the live event, then the unit will receive credit for the live event CRP only. If a tactical situation develops that precludes performing the live event, the unit would then receive credit for the simulation CRP.

1014. MARINE CORPS GROUND T&R PROGRAM

1. The Marine Corps Ground T&R Program continues to evolve. The vision for Ground T&R Program is to publish a T&R Manual for every readiness-reporting unit so that core capability METs are clearly defined with supporting collective training standards, and to publish community-based T&R Manuals for all occupational fields whose personnel augment other units to increase their combat and/or logistic capabilities. The vision for this program includes plans to provide a Marine Corps training management information system that enables tracking of unit and individual training accomplishments by unit commanders and small unit leaders, automatically computing CRP for both units and individual Marines based upon MOS and rank (or billet). Linkage of T&R Events to the Marine Corps Task List (MCTL), through the core capability METs, has enabled objective assessment of training readiness in the DRRS.

2. DRRS measures and reports on the readiness of military forces and the supporting infrastructure to meet missions and goals assigned by the Secretary of Defense. With unit CRP based on the unit's training toward its METs, the CRP will provide a more accurate picture of a unit's readiness. This will give fidelity to future funding requests and factor into the allocation of resources. Additionally, the Ground T&R Program will help to ensure training remains focused on mission accomplishment and that training readiness reporting is tied to units' METLs.

CHAPTER 2

MISSION ESSENTIAL TASKS MATRIX

MUSIC T&R MANUAL

CHAPTER 2

MISSION ESSENTIAL TASKS MATRIX

2000. MUSIC T&R MANUAL MISSION ESSENTIAL TASKS MATRIX. The Mission Essential Task List (METL) Table includes the designated MET number. The individual training standards in this T&R Manual were developed to support these METS.

MET 1.	**Provide musical support for military and civilian concerts**
MET 2.	**Provide musical support for civilian parades**
MET 3.	**Provide musical support for military and civilian ceremonies**
MET 4.	**Provide musical support for command sponsored social events**
MET 5.	**Provide internal support for band operations**

MUSIC T&R MANUAL

CHAPTER 3

COLLECTIVE EVENTS

CHAPTER 3

COLLECTIVE EVENTS

3000. PURPOSE. This chapter includes all collective events. These events are linked to a Service-Level Mission Essential Task (MET). This linkage tailor's collective and individual training for the selected MET. Each collective event is composed of component events that provide the major actions required. This may be likely actions, list of functions, or procedures. Accomplishment and proficiency level required of component events are determined by the event standard.

3001. ADMINISTRATIVE NOTES

1.   T&R events are coded for ease of reference. Each event has a 4-4-4 digit identifier. The first four digits represent the occupational field, "MUSC". The second four digits represent the functional or duty area. The last four digits represent the level, and identifier number of the event. The MUSIC collective training events are only in the 4000 and 5000 levels. Every event has a unique identifier number from 001 to 999.

2.   The MUSIC collective training events are:

    4000 Level - for Jazz Ensemble, Show Band, Combo and Small Ensembles
    5000 Level - for Concert and Ceremonial Bands

3.   The functional areas for the MUSIC collective events are:

    PERF - Performance
    SUPT - Support

3002. 4000-LEVEL COLLECTIVE EVENTS DESCRIPTION

1. Jazz Ensemble. The jazz ensemble performs jazz, which includes swing, Latin, and all contemporary styles. This unit has 15 to 20 members. Standard instrumentation calls for Saxophone, Trumpet, Trombone, Percussion, Electric Bass, Piano, and Guitar. Music amplification must be considered as an integral part of the instrumentation of this ensemble to enhance the sound, compensate for poor acoustics, provide for announcements, and amplify solos.

2. Show Band. The show band performs rock, pop, and other contemporary music styles. This unit has five to 15 members. Standard instrumentation calls for Keyboard, Guitar, Electric Bass, Percussion, and Vocals. A horn section including Saxophone, Trumpet, and Trombone may be added as appropriate for the music being performed. Music amplification must be considered as an integral part of the instrumentation of this ensemble to enhance the sound, compensate for poor acoustics, provide for announcements, and to amplify solos.

3. Small Ensembles. Small ensembles (party band, quintets, quartets, trios, piano soloists, etc.) provide music for official military and civilian missions. These ensembles provide an alternative to the larger musical units within the band in those cases where limited space, funds or transportation are a factor or when particular musical considerations would render a smaller ensemble more appropriate or effective and provide for training opportunities.

4. Combo. The combo performs jazz, swing, rock and other styles of popular music. This ensemble is normally comprised of three to eight musicians, and requires the use of amplification to achieve the characteristic sound expected by audiences. Soloists, when available, require amplification to be heard and blend with the ensemble.

3003. 5000-LEVEL COLLECTIVE EVENTS DESCRIPTION

1. Concert Band. The concert band performs all types of traditional band music and transcriptions. This group uses all the musicians assigned to the unit and may include members of the band's command element. The concert band is normally led by the band officer. Music amplification and recording equipment is normally used during concert band rehearsals and performances to enhance sound, compensate for poor acoustics, to record performances, as well as provide for announcements, introductions and narrations.

2. Ceremonial Band. The ceremonial band performs official ceremonial music, marches, patriotic music, and is the primary ceremonial unit. This unit normally has 44 members. Typically, musicians who perform Oboe, Bassoon, Electric Bass, Piano and Electric Guitar are not assigned to this ensemble. If manning shortfalls are critical, these musicians can perform a secondary instrument in the band (MCO P1200.7).

3004. INDEX OF 4000-LEVEL COLLECTIVE EVENTS BY FUNCTIONAL AREA

EVENT	DESCRIPTION	PAGE
	PERFORMANCE	
MUSC-PERF-4001	Perform small ensemble concert	3-5
	SUPPORT	
MUSC-SUPT-4010	Maintain Administrative Section	3-5
MUSC-SUPT-4011	Maintain Library Section	3-6
MUSC-SUPT-4012	Maintain Marketing/Public Affairs Section	3-7
MUSC-SUPT-4013	Maintain Audio/Visual Section	3-8
MUSC-SUPT-4014	Maintain Supply Section	3-8
MUSC-SUPT-4015	Maintain Loading Section	3-9

3005. INDEX OF 5000-LEVEL COLLECTIVE EVENTS BY FUNCTIONAL AREA

EVENT	DESCRIPTION	PAGE
	PERFORMANCE	
MUSC-PERF-5001	Perform field drill	3-11
MUSC-PERF-5002	Perform ceremonial music	3-11
MUSC-PERF-5003	Perform concert band music	3-12

3006. 4000-LEVEL COLLECTIVE EVENTS

MUSC-PERF-4001: Perform small ensemble concert

SUPPORTED MET(S): 1, 3, 4

EVALUATION-CODED: NO   **SUSTAINMENT INTERVAL**: 12 months

DESCRIPTION: Required small ensembles are defined in MCO P5000.18_ Marine Corps Band Manual.

CONDITION: Given an approved commitment request, an equipped small ensemble, designated music, and appropriate performance venue.

STANDARD: To ensure a musical program appropriate for the venue, audience, and occasion per industry standards.

EVENT COMPONENTS:
1. Provide internal support for Band operations.
2. Rehearse small ensemble music.
3. Conduct onsite preparation for performance.
4. Execute performance.

REFERENCE:
1. MCO P5000.18_ Marine Corps Band Manual

SUPPORT REQUIREMENTS:

  TRANSPORTATION: Provide appropriate aircraft, buses, equipment trucks, or vans to transport all personnel and equipment from home station to performance location.

  ROOMS/BUILDINGS: An appropriate performance facility/venue.

  EQUIPMENT: Appropriate musical instruments, musical equipment, sound reinforcement and audio and video recording equipment.

  MATERIAL: Appropriate sheet music and musical supplies.

  UNITS/PERSONNEL: Support personnel, as required.

MUSC-SUPT-4010: Maintain Administrative Section

SUPPORTED MET(S): 1, 2, 3, 4, 5

EVALUATION-CODED: NO   **SUSTAINMENT INTERVAL**: 12 months

CONDITION: Given assigned band personnel, operations plan, commitment and training schedule.

STANDARD: To ensure all organizational, operational and administrative requirements are fulfilled in accordance with MCO P5000.18_.

EVENT COMPONENTS:
1. Process naval correspondence.
2. Process naval messages.
3. Manage correspondence files.
4. Manage Directives Control Point.
5. Review command issued directives.

REFERENCES:
1. MCO P5000.18_ Marine Corps Band Manual
2. OPNAVINST 4631.2 D Management of Department of the Navy (DON) Airlift Assets
3. SECNAVINST 5216.5 W/CH 1-2 Department of the Navy (DON) Correspondence Manual
4. SECNAVINST M-5210.2 Standard Subject Identification Codes
5. Local SOPs
6. UFC 4-171-04AN Department of Defense Design Guide - Band Training Facilities

SUPPORT REQUIREMENTS:

ROOMS/BUILDINGS: An appropriate meeting and records storage facility.

EQUIPMENT: Appropriate computer and support equipment.

MATERIAL: Appropriate logistical and administrative supplies.

UNITS/PERSONNEL: Detachment of band personnel.

MUSC-SUPT-4011: Maintain Library Section

SUPPORTED MET(S): 1, 2, 3, 4, 5

EVALUATION-CODED: NO   **SUSTAINMENT INTERVAL:** 12 months

CONDITION: Given assigned band personnel, required library materials, sheet music, music texts, reference materials, and music publications.

STANDARD: To ensure all required music materials are on hand, current, properly accounted for, and maintained in an organized manner.

EVENT COMPONENTS:
1. Issue music publications to Band personnel, as necessary.
2. Request new publication purchases from band supply section.
3. Maintain updated inventory of all required music publications.
4. Maintain performance log.

REFERENCES:
1. BYRNE, FRANK PRACTICAL GUIDE TO THE MUSIC LIBRARY: ITS FUNCTION, ORGANIZATION AND MAINTENANCE; Publisher: Ludwig Music Company (December 1987)
2. MCO P5000.18_ Marine Corps Band Manual

3. UFC 4-171-04AN Department of Defense Design Guide - Band Training
    Facilities
4. PUBLIC LAW 94 553 Federal copyright Act, Title 17 of the U.S. Code

SUPPORT REQUIREMENTS:

ROOMS/BUILDINGS: An appropriate meeting and storage facility.

EQUIPMENT: Appropriate computer equipment, computer support, and storage
equipment.

MATERIALS: Appropriate logistical and administrative supplies.

UNITS/PERSONNEL: Detachment of Band personnel.

MUSC-SUPT-4012: Maintain Marketing/Public Affairs Section

SUPPORTED MET(S): 1, 2, 3, 4, 5

EVALUATION-CODED: NO   SUSTAINMENT INTERVAL: 12 months

CONDITION: Given assigned band personnel, an operational plan, the command's
concept of operations for surrounding communities, and approved commitments.

STANDARD: To enhance community awareness by providing accurate and timely
information of unit's operations to maximize attendance at public performances.

EVENT COMPONENTS:
1. Liaise with command Public Affairs Office (PAO).
2. Liaise with appropriate Marine Corps District (MCD) Musician Technical
    Assistant (MTA) upon scheduling of commitment.
3. Liaise with appropriate MCD Public Affairs (PA) Representative upon
    scheduling of commitment.
4. Liaise with appropriate local recruiter upon scheduling of commitment.
5. Maintain band web site.
6. Maintain Band press packages.
7. Populate www.marines.mil "In the Community" calendar with all public
    performance information.

REFERENCES:
1. MCO 5726.15 Marine Corps Band Support of Community Relations
2. MCO P5000.18_ Marine Corps Band Manual
3. MCO P5750.1G W/CH 1 Manual for the Marine Corps Historical Program
4. SECNAVINST 5720.44B Public Affairs Policy and Regulations
5. UFC 4-171-04AN Department of Defense Design Guide - Band Training
    Facilities
6. StratCom - Strategic Communication Plan, PCN 50100654400, dtd July 2007

SUPPORT REQUIREMENTS:

ROOMS/BUILDINGS: An appropriate meeting and storage facility.

EQUIPMENT: Appropriate computer equipment, computer support, and digital photography equipment.

MATERIAL: Appropriate press packages, photographs, band historical records, administrative, and logistical supplies.

UNITS/PERSONNEL: Detachment of band personnel.

MUSC-SUPT-4013: Maintain Audio/Visual Section

SUPPORTED MET(S): 1, 2, 3, 4, 5

EVALUATION-CODED: NO   **SUSTAINMENT INTERVAL**: 12 months

DESCRIPTION: This Section maintains both sound reinforcement and audio/visual recording capabilities in both live performances and rehearsals.

CONDITION: Given sound reinforcement and audio/visual recording requirements, designated ensemble, proper equipment, sound crew, and performance venue.

STANDARD: To ensure industry standard quality sound reinforcement and audio/visual recordings.

EVENT COMPONENTS:
1. Operate audio/visual equipment as required.
2. Provide recorded music to sponsor upon non-availability of live musical support.

REFERENCES:
1. FABER, S. RECORDING HANDBOOK
2. MCO P5000.18B Marine Corps Band Manual
3. STARK, S. H. LIVE SOUND REINFORCEMENT
4. UFC 4-171-04AN Department of Defense Design Guide - Band Training Facilities

SUPPORT REQUIREMENTS:

ROOMS/BUILDINGS: An acoustically designed recording studio and appropriate performance venue.

EQUIPMENT: Industry standard computer equipment, peripherals, software, sound reinforcement, and audio recording equipment capable of producing high quality digital audio/visual recordings.

MATERIAL: Appropriate pre-recorded and blank media, administrative, and logistical supplies.

UNITS/PERSONNEL: Detachment of Band personnel.

MUSC-SUPT-4014: Maintain Supply Section

SUPPORTED MET(S): 1, 2, 3, 4, 5

EVALUATION-CODED: NO   **SUSTAINMENT INTERVAL**: 12 months

CONDITION: Given an annual budget, music materials/publications sources, supply personnel, administrative supplies, inventory record, and computer.

STANDARD: To ensure all required instruments, band equipment, music, publications, and support equipment are on hand, current, and properly procured and controlled.

EVENT COMPONENTS:
1. Issue musical instruments/band equipment.
2. Maintain appropriate inventory for mission capabilities.
3. Procure musical materials/publications.
4. Procure musical instruments/band equipment.
5. Procure organizational clothing/equipment.
6. Procure support equipment as required.
7. Procure maintenance/repair equipment.
8. Maintain regular accountability of equipment listed on the unit's Consolidated Memorandum Receipt.

REFERENCES:
1. 29 CFR 1910.95 Occupational Safety and Health Standards - Occupational noise exposure
2. MCO 5100.8 Marine Corps Occupational Safety and Health (OSH) Policy Order
3. MCO P4200.15 Marine Corps Purchasing Procedures Manual
4. MCO P4400.150E W/ERRATUM CH 1-2 Consumer Level Policy Manual
5. MCO P5000.18B Marine Corps Band Manual
6. UFC 4-171-04AN Department of Defense Design Guide - Band Training Facilities

SUPPORT REQUIREMENTS:

  ROOMS/BUILDINGS: A climate-controlled secure storage environment.

  EQUIPMENT: Appropriate musical instruments, appropriate musical equipment, administrative equipment and computer.

  MATERIAL: Appropriate musical supplies, band instrument catalogs, supply catalogs, instrument repairs catalogs, music publication catalogs, and administrative and logistical supplies.

  UNITS/PERSONNEL: A detachment of Band personnel.

MUSC-SUPT-4015: Maintain Loading Section

SUPPORTED MET(S): 1, 2, 3, 4, 5

EVALUATION-CODED: NO   **SUSTAINMENT INTERVAL**: 12 months

CONDITION: Given a mode of transportation, equipment, and loading crew.

STANDARD: To ensure all required equipment is efficiently loaded in a safe manner with 100% accuracy.

EVENT COMPONENTS:
1. Liaise with unit leader.
2. Create manifest.
3. Load/unload equipment.

REFERENCES:
1. MCO 5100.8 Marine Corps Occupational Safety and Health (OSH) Policy Order
2. MCO P5000.18_ Marine Corps Band Manual
3. MCO 3500.27_ Operational Risk Management

SUPPORT REQUIREMENTS:

ROOMS/BUILDINGS: Securable storage area.

EQUIPMENT: Appropriate Personal Protective Equipment and necessary equipment securing devices.

UNITS/PERSONNEL: A detachment of Band personnel.

3007. 5000-LEVEL COLLECTIVE EVENTS

MUSC-PERF-5001: Perform field drill

SUPPORTED MET(S): 1, 2, 3, 4

EVALUATION-CODED: NO   SUSTAINMENT INTERVAL: 12 months

CONDITION: Given assigned personnel, in appropriately designed performance space with required musical equipment, designated sequence, and designated music.

STANDARD: To ensure a musical program appropriate for the venue, audience, and occasion, and per industry standards.

EVENT COMPONENTS:
1. Provide internal support for Band operations.
2. Rehearse field drill.
3. Conduct on-site preparation for performance.
4. Execute performance plan.

REFERENCES:
1. MCO P5000.18_ Marine Corps Band Manual
2. MCO P5060.20 Marine Corps Drill and Ceremonies Manual
3. U. S. Navy Regulations - Chapter 12 - Flags, Pennants, Honors, Ceremonies, and Customs

SUPPORT REQUIREMENTS:

  TRANSPORTATION: Provide appropriate aircraft, buses, equipment trucks, or vans to transport all personnel and equipment from home station to performance location.

  ROOMS/BUILDINGS: An appropriate performance facility or area.

  EQUIPMENT: Appropriate musical instruments, musical equipment, and video recording equipment as required.

  MATERIAL: Appropriate sheet music and logistical supplies.

  UNITS/PERSONNEL: All Band personnel, as required.

MUSC-PERF-5002: Perform ceremonial music

SUPPORTED MET(S): 1, 2, 3, 4

EVALUATION-CODED: NO   SUSTAINMENT INTERVAL: 12 months

CONDITION: Given assigned personnel in appropriately designed performance space with required musical equipment, designated sequence, and designated music.

STANDARD: To ensure a musical program appropriate for the venue, audience, and occasion, and per industry standards.

EVENT COMPONENTS:
1. Provide internal support for Band operations.
2. Rehearse ceremonial music.
3. Conduct on-site preparation for performance.
4. Execute performance plan.

REFERENCES:
1. MCO P5000.18_ Marine Corps Band Manual
2. MCO P5060.20 Marine Corps Drill and Ceremonies Manual
3. U. S. Navy Regulations w/Ch 1 Chapter 12 - Flags, Pennants, Honors, Ceremonies, and Customs

SUPPORT REQUIREMENTS:

TRANSPORTATION: Provide appropriate aircraft, buses, equipment trucks, or vans to transport all personnel and equipment from home station to performance location.

ROOMS/BUILDINGS: An appropriate performance facility or area.

EQUIPMENT: Appropriate musical instruments, musical equipment, and video recording equipment as required.

MATERIAL: Appropriate sheet music and logistical supplies.

UNITS/PERSONNEL: All Band personnel, as required.

MUSC-PERF-5003: Perform Concert Band music

SUPPORTED MET(S): 1, 3, 4

EVALUATION-CODED: NO   **SUSTAINMENT INTERVAL**: 12 months

CONDITION: Given assigned personnel, in appropriately designed performance space with required musical equipment, designated sequence, and designated music.

STANDARD: To ensure a musical program appropriate for the venue, audience, and occasion, and per industry standards.

EVENT COMPONENTS:
1. Provide internal support for Band operations.
2. Rehearse Concert Band.
3. Conduct on-site preparation for performance.
4. Execute performance plan.

REFERENCE:
1. MCO P5000.18B Marine Corps Band Manual

SUPPORT REQUIREMENTS:

TRANSPORTATION: Provide appropriate aircraft, buses, equipment trucks, or vans to transport all personnel and equipment from home station to performance location.

ROOMS/BUILDINGS: An appropriate performance facility or area.

EQUIPMENT: Appropriate musical instruments, musical equipment, and video recording equipment as required.

MATERIAL: Appropriate sheet music and logistical supplies.

UNITS/PERSONNEL: All Band personnel, as required.

MUSIC T&R MANUAL

CHAPTER 4

MOS 5502 INDIVIDUAL EVENTS

CHAPTER 4

MOS 5502 INDIVIDUAL EVENTS

4000. PURPOSE. This chapter details the individual events that pertain to occupational field 55, Music. These events are linked to a service-level Mission Essential Tasks (MET). This linkage tailors individual training for the selected MET. Each individual event provides an event title, along with the conditions events will be performed under, and the standard to which the event must be performed to be successful.

4001. ADMINISTRATIVE NOTES. T&R events are coded for ease of reference. Events in the T&R Manual are depicted with a 12 field alphanumeric system, i.e. 5502-ADMN-2001. This chapter utilizes the following methodology:

a. The first four digits represent the occupational field or military occupational field (e.g., Occupational Field 55 or Band Officer MOS 5502). This chapter contains 5502 events.

b. The second four alpha characters represent the functional or duty area (e.g., ADMN - Administration). Functional areas for Band Officers are:

```
ADMN - Administration
AUDN - Audition
CREL - Community Relations
FISC - Fiscal
PERF - Performance
PLAN - Planning
SUPT - Support
```

c. The last four digits represent the task level and numerical sequencing. The Music individual training events are separated into two task levels:

```
1000 - Core Skills (initial MOS training conducted at formal schools)
2000 - Core Plus Skills (follow-on formal schooling, MOJT or distance
       learning)
```

Every individual event has a numerical identifier from 001 to 999.

d. The individual task condition statement sets forth the real-world circumstances in which the task is to be performed. Condition statements describe the equipment, tools, materials, environmental or safety considerations, and resources need to perform the task and the assistance, location, etc. that relates to performance of the task. In a garrison or field environment and with the aid of references are common conditions for all Occupational Field 55 tasks unless otherwise noted.

4002. INDEX OF INDIVIDUAL EVENTS

1. **2000-LEVEL EVENTS.** There are no 1000-level individual events for Band Officers. 2000-level individual events for Band Officers are taught at either follow-on school, by MOJT or through Distance Learning. Special Note: the events with an asterisk denote tasks which are <u>initially</u> taught in the Senior Musician and the Unit Leader Courses which are pre-requisites for selection to MOS 5502, Band Officer. They may also be considered MOJT upon a Band Officer's assignment to the operating forces and supporting establishment.

EVENT	DESCRIPTION	PAGE
	ADMINISTRATION	
5502-ADMN-2001*	Direct Band Leadership	4-4
5502-ADMN-2002	Submit Band command chronology	4-4
5502-ADMN-2003	Write commitment After Action Report	4-4
	AUDITION	
5502-AUDN-2010*	Audition personnel	4-5
5502-AUDN-2011*	Audition prospective applicant	4-5
	COMMUNITY RELATIONS	
5502-CREL-2020*	Deliver Marine Corps Band marketing presentation	4-6
	FISCAL	
5502-FISC-2040	Approve submission of annual budget	4-7
5502-FISC-2041	Reconcile Consolidated Memorandum of Receipt (CMR)	4-7
5502-FISC-2042	Approve Periodic Replacement Plan (PRP)	4-8
	PERFORMANCE	
5502-PERF-2050*	Lead Band in performance	4-8
	PLANNING	
5502-PLAN-2060	Approve annual operational plan	4-9
5502-PLAN-2061	Approve Band schedule	4-9
5502-PLAN-2062	Assign commitment request disposition	4-10
	SUPPORT	
5502-SUPT-2070	Approve purchase requests	4-10

4003. 2000-LEVEL EVENTS

5502-ADMN-2001*: Direct Band Leadership

EVALUATION-CODED: NO   **SUSTAINMENT INTERVAL:** 12 months

BILLETS: Band Officer

GRADES: WO-1, CWO-2, CWO-3, CWO-4, CWO-5

INITIAL TRAINING SETTING: FORMAL

CONDITION: Given Band personnel.

STANDARD: To ensure all assigned areas remain 100% mission capable.

PERFORMANCE STEPS:
1. Communicate commander's intent to Band leadership.
2. Evaluate execution of commander's intent.
3. Mentor assigned personnel.

REFERENCE:
1. MCO P5000.18_ Marine Corps Band Manual

5502-ADMN-2002: Submit Band command chronology

EVALUATION-CODED: NO   **SUSTAINMENT INTERVAL:** 12 months

BILLETS: Band Officer

GRADES: WO-1, CWO-2, CWO-3, CWO-4, CWO-5

INITIAL TRAINING SETTING: MOJT

CONDITION: Given a draft Band command chronology.

STANDARD: To accurately capture the past operations of the unit.

PERFORMANCE STEPS:
1. Review draft command chronology.
2. Forward signed command chronology to higher headquarters.

REFERENCES:
1. MCO P5000.18B Marine Corps Band Manual
2. MCO P5750.1G W/CH 1 Manual for the Marine Corps Historical Program

---

5502-ADMN-2003: Write commitment After Action Report

EVALUATION-CODED: NO   **SUSTAINMENT INTERVAL:** 12 months

BILLETS: Band Officer

GRADES: WO-1, CWO-2, CWO-3, CWO-4, CWO-5

INITIAL TRAINING SETTING: MOJT

CONDITION: Given a blank After Action Report form and commitment folder pertaining to a completed commitment.

STANDARD: Within seven days, ensuring the report is 100% accurate and complete.

PERFORMANCE STEPS:
1. Review personal notes pertaining to commitment.
2. Review commitment folder for additional information, as required.
3. Complete appropriate After Action Report form.
4. Submit completed After Action Report, with commitment folder, to Bandmaster.

REFERENCES:
1. MCO 5726.15 Marine Corps Band Support of Community Relations
2. MCO P5000.18_ Marine Corps Band Manual
3. SECNAVINST 5720.44B Public Affairs Policy and Regulations

5502-AUDN-2010*: Audition personnel

EVALUATION-CODED: NO   SUSTAINMENT INTERVAL: 6 months

BILLETS: Band Officer

GRADES: WO-1, CWO-2, CWO-3, CWO-4, CWO-5

INITIAL TRAINING SETTING: FORMAL

CONDITION: Given an instrumentalist with instrument, music stand, audition book, administrative materials, copy of auditionee's solo, metronome, and designated location.

STANDARD: In performance step sequence, to ascertain technical proficiency and ensuring 98% accuracy and consistency with the Audition Standards Manual.

PERFORMANCE STEPS:
1. Grade prepared material.
2. Grade performance of rudiments or scales.
3. Grade performance of sight reading material.
4. Average numerical score for all criteria.
5. Evaluate memorized music as required.

REFERENCES:
1. MCO P5000.18_ Marine Corps Band Manual
2. MUSCOLINST 1300.1 Audition Standards Manual

5502-AUDN-2011*: Audition prospective applicant

EVALUATION-CODED: NO   **SUSTAINMENT INTERVAL**: 6 months

BILLETS: Band Officer

GRADES: WO-1, CWO-2, CWO-3, CWO-4, CWO-5

INITIAL TRAINING SETTING: FORMAL

CONDITION: Given a prospective Marine musician applicant with instrument, music stand, audition book, administrative materials, an audition form, a MEOP screening form, copy of auditionee's solo, metronome, designated location, and in a garrison environment.

STANDARD: In performance step sequence, to ascertain technical proficiency and ensuring 98% accuracy and consistency with the Audition Standards Manual.

PERFORMANCE STEPS:
1. Screen prospective applicant.
2. Establish rapport with applicant.
3. Establish proper audition environment.
4. Determine if prepared solo meets required difficulty level.
5. Review auditions process with applicant.
6. Provide warm-up opportunity, if required.
7. Evaluate auditionee's competency by observing musical criteria demonstrated.
8. Describe each criterion observed in descriptive adjectives criteria form.
9. Record numerical score for each criterion that most accurately corresponds to descriptive adjective.
10. Average numerical score for all criteria.
11. Record final average in appropriate block on audition form.
12. Counsel auditionee on final results.
13. File copy of audition form.
14. Forward results, as required.

REFERENCES:
1. MCO P5000.18_ Marine Corps Band Manual
2. MUSCOLINST 1300.1 Audition Standards Manual
3. MCO 1200.17_Military Occupational Specialties Manual

5502-CREL-2020*: Deliver Marine Corps Band marketing presentation

EVALUATION-CODED: NO   **SUSTAINMENT INTERVAL**: 12 months

BILLETS: Band Officer

GRADES: WO-1, CWO-2, CWO-3, CWO-4, CWO-5

INITIAL TRAINING SETTING: FORMAL

CONDITION: Given a targeted audience, current Band information, and computer with presentation software.

STANDARD: To clearly and concisely address current leadership and performance opportunities within Marine Corps Bands.

PERFORMANCE STEPS:
1. Schedule presentation.
2. Gather demographic information on civilian musical unit.
3. Prepare presentation outline.
4. Rehearse presentation outline.
5. Deliver presentation.
6. Answer questions.
7. Provide feedback to Marine Corps Recruiting Command.

REFERENCES:
1. MCO 1130.53P w/CH 1 Enlistment Incentive Programs
2. MCO 5726.15 Marine Corps Band Support of Community Relations
3. MCO P5000.18_ Marine Corps Band Manual
4. MCRC VOLUME 3-Guidebook for Recruiting Station Operations
5. PUBLIC LAW 94-553 Federal Copyright Act, Title 17 of U.S. Code

---

5502-FISC-2040: Approve submission of annual budget

EVALUATION-CODED: NO   **SUSTAINMENT INTERVAL**: 12 months

BILLETS: Band Officer

GRADES: WO-1, CWO-2, CWO-3, CWO-4, CWO-5

INITIAL TRAINING SETTING: MOJT

CONDITION: Given a draft budget submission.

STANDARD: Ensuring all funding requirements and deficiencies are identified.

PERFORMANCE STEPS:
1. Review annual budget draft.
2. Make any necessary adjustments.
3. Submit budget to higher headquarters.

REFERENCES:
1. MCO 4400.163 DoD Supply Management Reference Book (Jan 85)
2. MCO P4400.150E W/ERRATUM CH 1-2 Consumer Level Policy Manual (Jun 99)
3. MCO P5000.18B Marine Corps Band Manual
4. MCO P7100.8K Field Budget Guidance Manual

5502-FISC-2041: Reconcile Consolidated Memorandum of Receipt (CMR)

EVALUATION-CODED: NO   **SUSTAINMENT INTERVAL**: 12 months

BILLETS: Band Officer

GRADES: WO-1, CWO-2, CWO-3, CWO-4, CWO-5

INITIAL TRAINING SETTING: MOJT

CONDITION: Given a current CMR.

STANDARD: To ensure 100% accountability for Band equipment.

PERFORMANCE STEPS:
1. Inventory all CMR items.
2. Identify administrative errors.
3. Draft letter of discrepancy.
4. Sign reconciled CMR with Supply Officer.

REFERENCES:
1. MCO 4340.1A W/CH 1 Reporting Missing, Lost, Stolen, or Recovered (MLSR) Government Property
2. MCO 4400.163 DoD Supply Management Reference Book
3. MCO P5000.18B Marine Corps Band Manual
4. UM 4400-15 Organic Property Control

5502-FISC-2042: Approve Periodic Replacement Plan (PRP)

EVALUATION-CODED: NO   **SUSTAINMENT INTERVAL**: 12 months

BILLETS: Band Officer

GRADES: WO-1, CWO-2, CWO-3, CWO-4, CWO-5

INITIAL TRAINING SETTING: MOJT

CONDITION: Given a Table of Organization and Equipment (TO&E) and current Consolidated Memorandum of Receipt (CMR).

STANDARD: Ensuring all TO&E requirements and deficiencies are properly identified to include cost estimates by year.

PERFORMANCE STEPS:
1. Receive proposed PRP from Instrument Repair Technician.
2. Make necessary adjustments to proposed PRP.

REFERENCES:
1. MCO P5000.18_ Marine Corps Band Manual

5502-PERF-2050*: Lead Band in performance

EVALUATION-CODED: NO   **SUSTAINMENT INTERVAL**: 12 months

BILLETS: Band Officer

GRADES: WO-1, CWO-2, CWO-3, CWO-4, CWO-5

INITIAL TRAINING SETTING: FORMAL

CONDITION: Given a baton, a fully equipped Band, and a performance venue.

STANDARD: Directing and rehearsing Concert and Ceremonial Bands at a 3.0 level.

PERFORMANCE STEPS:
1. Brief the sequence of events to ensemble.
2. Direct ensemble using proper techniques.
3. Correct music in rehearsal as appropriate.
4. Execute sequence of events.
5. Program appropriate music.

REFERENCES:
1. MCO P5000.18_ Marine Corps Band Manual
2. MCO P5060.20_ Marine Corps Drill and Ceremonies Manual
3. U. S. Navy Regulations w/Ch 1, Chapter 12 - Flags, Pennants, Honors, Ceremonies, and Customs

---

5502-PLAN-2060: Approve annual operational plan

EVALUATION-CODED: NO   **SUSTAINMENT INTERVAL**: 12 months

BILLETS: Band Officer

GRADES: WO-1, CWO-2, CWO-3, CWO-4, CWO-5

INITIAL TRAINING SETTING: MOJT

CONDITION: Given a draft annual operational plan.

STANDARD: Ensure all national and local support requirements and periods of non-availability are reflected.

PERFORMANCE STEPS:
1. Review draft for accuracy.
2. Reconcile conflicts.
3. Sign for publication.

REFERENCES:
1. MCO 5726.15 Marine Corps Band Support of Community Relations
2. MCO P5000.18B Marine Corps Band Manual
3. StratCom - Strategic Communication Plan, PCN 50100654400, dated July 2007

5502-PLAN-2061: Approve Band schedule

EVALUATION-CODED: NO   **SUSTAINMENT INTERVAL**: 12 months

BILLETS: Band Officer

GRADES: WO-1, CWO-2, CWO-3, CWO-4, CWO-5

INITIAL TRAINING SETTING: MOJT

CONDITION: Given a draft band schedule.

STANDARD: Ensure all training requirements are met and the unit remains mission capable for all approved commitments.

PERFORMANCE STEPS:
1. Review draft for accuracy.
2. Reconcile conflicts.
3. Sign for publication.

REFERENCE:
1. MCO P5000.18_ Marine Corps Band Manual

5502-PLAN-2062: Assign commitment request disposition

EVALUATION-CODED: NO   **SUSTAINMENT INTERVAL**: 12 months

BILLETS: Band Officer

GRADES: WO-1, CWO-2, CWO-3, CWO-4, CWO-5

INITIAL TRAINING SETTING: MOJT

CONDITION: Given a commitment request, annual operation plan, Band schedule, and funding requirements.

STANDARD: To accurately determine feasibility of support.

PERFORMANCE STEPS:
1. Review Bandmaster's recommendation.
2. Review the Band schedule
3. Approve or disapprove as appropriate.

REFERENCES:
1. MCO 5726.15 Marine Corps Band Support of Community Relations
2. MCO P5000.18_ Marine Corps Band Manual
3. SECNAVINST 5720.44B Public Affairs Policy and Regulations
4. Local Standard Operating Procedures

5502-SUPT-2070: Approve purchase requests

EVALUATION-CODED: NO   **SUSTAINMENT INTERVAL**: 12 months

BILLETS: Band Officer

GRADES: WO-1, CWO-2, CWO-3, CWO-4, CWO-5

INITIAL TRAINING SETTING: MOJT

CONDITION: Given a draft purchase request.

STANDARD: To ensure requested materials meet all TO&E requirements.

PERFORMANCE STEPS:
1.   Review draft purchase request.
2.   Authorize purchase request.

REFERENCE:
2.   MCO P5000.18_ Marine Corps Band Manual

CHAPTER 5

MOS 5519 INDIVIDUAL EVENTS

MUSIC T&R MANUAL

CHAPTER 5

MOS 5519 INDIVIDUAL EVENTS

5000. PURPOSE. This chapter details the individual events that pertain to the occupational field 55, Music. These events are linked to a service-level Mission Essential Tasks (MET). This linkage tailors individual training for the selected MET. Each individual event provides an event title, along with the conditions events will be performed under, and the standard to which the event must be performed to be successful.

5001. ADMINISTRATIVE NOTES. T&R events are coded for ease of reference. Events in the T&R manual are depicted with a 12 field alphanumeric system, i.e. 5519-ADMN-2002. This chapter utilizes the following methodology:

a. The first four digits represent the occupational field or military occupational field (e.g., Occupational Field 55 or Enlisted Conductor MOS 5519). This chapter contains 5519 events.

b. The second four alpha characters represent the functional or duty area (e.g., CREL – Community Relations). Functional areas for Enlisted Conductors are:

    ADMN – Administration
    AUDN – Audition
    CREL – Community Relations
    PERF – Performance
    PLAN – Planning
    TRNG – Training

c. The last four digits represent the task level and numerical sequencing. The Music individual training events are separated into two task levels:

    1000 – Core Skills (initial MOS training conducted at formal schools)
    2000 – Core Plus Skills (follow-on formal schooling, MOJT or distance
           learning)

Every individual event has a numerical identifier from 001 to 999.

d. The individual task condition statement sets forth the real-world circumstances in which the task is to be performed. Condition statements describe the equipment, tools, materials, environmental or safety considerations, and resources need to perform the task and the assistance, location, etc. that relates to performance of the task. In a garrison or field environment and with the aid of references are common conditions for all Occupational Field 55 tasks unless otherwise noted.

5002. INDEX OF INDIVIDUAL EVENTS

1. **2000-LEVEL EVENTS.** There are no 1000-level individual events for Enlisted Conductors. 2000-level individual events for Enlisted Conductors are taught at follow-on schools, by MOJT or through Distance Learning.

ADMINISTRATION		
5519-ADMN-2001	Manage assigned logistical areas	5-4
AUDITION		
5519-ADMN-2010	Audition personnel	5-4
COMMUNITY RELATIONS		
5519-CREL-2020	Deliver Marine Corps Band marketing presentation	5-5
PERFORMANCE		
5519-PERF-2050	Lead Ceremonial Band	5-5
PLANNING		
5519-PLAN-2060	Coordinate support for commitments	5-6
TRAINING		
5519-SUPT-2080	Manage musician development	5-6

5003. 2000-LEVEL EVENTS

5519-ADMN-2001: Manage assigned logistical areas

EVALUATION-CODED: NO   **SUSTAINMENT INTERVAL**: 12 months

BILLETS: Enlisted Conductor

GRADES: SSGT, GYSGT

INITIAL TRAINING SETTING: MOJT

CONDITION: Given band personnel.

STANDARD: Ensuring all assigned areas remain 100% mission capable.

PERFORMANCE STEPS:
1. Oversee Library Section.
2. Oversee Marketing/Public Affairs Section.
3. Train assigned personnel.

REFERENCE:
1. MCO P5000.18_ Marine Corps Band Manual

5519-AUDN-2010: Audition personnel

EVALUATION-CODED: NO   **SUSTAINMENT INTERVAL**: 6 months

BILLETS: Enlisted Conductor

GRADES: SSGT, GYSGT

INITIAL TRAINING SETTING: FORMAL

CONDITION: Given an instrumentalist with instrument, music stand, audition book, administrative materials, copy of auditionee's solo, metronome, and designated location.

STANDARD: In performance step sequence, to ascertain technical proficiency and ensuring 98% accuracy and consistency with the Audition Standards Manual.

PERFORMANCE STEPS:
1. Grade prepared material.
2. Grade performance of rudiments or scales.
3. Grade performance of sight reading material.
4. Average numerical score for all criteria.
5. Evaluate memorized music as required.

REFERENCES:
1. MCO P5000.18_ Marine Corps Band Manual
2. MUSCOLINST 1300.1 Audition Standards

5519-CREL-2020: Deliver Marine Corps Band marketing presentation

EVALUATION-CODED: NO   **SUSTAINMENT INTERVAL**: 12 months

BILLETS: Enlisted Conductor

GRADES: SSGT, GYSGT

INITIAL TRAINING SETTING: FORMAL

CONDITION: Given a targeted audience, current Band information, and computer with presentation software.

STANDARD: To clearly and concisely address current leadership and performance opportunities within Marine Corps Bands.

PERFORMANCE STEPS:
1. Schedule presentation.
2. Gather demographic information on civilian musical unit.
3. Prepare presentation outline.
4. Rehearse presentation outline.
5. Deliver presentation.
6. Answer questions.
7. Provide feedback to Marine Corps Recruiting Command.

REFERENCES:
1. MCO 1130.53P w/Ch 1 Enlistment Incentive Programs
2. MCO 5726.15 Marine Corps Band Support of Community Relations
3. MCO P5000.18_ Marine Corps Band Manual
4. MCRC VOLUME 3-Guidebook for Recruiting Station Operations

5519-PERF-2050: Lead Ceremonial Band

EVALUATION-CODED: NO   **SUSTAINMENT INTERVAL**: 12 months

BILLETS: Enlisted Conductor

GRADES: SSGT, GYSGT

INITIAL TRAINING SETTING: FORMAL

CONDITION: Given a baton, a fully equipped band, and a performance venue.

STANDARD: Directing and rehearsing the Ceremonial Band at a 3.0 level.

PERFORMANCE STEPS:
1. Brief the sequence of events to ensemble.
2. Direct ensemble using proper techniques.
3. Correct music in rehearsal as appropriate.
4. Execute sequence of events.
5. Program appropriate music.

REFERENCES:
1. MCO P5000.18_ Marine Corps Band Manual
2. MCO P5060.20_ Marine Corps Drill and Ceremonies Manual
3. U.S. Navy Regulations w/Ch 1 Chapter 12 - Flags, Pennants, Honors, Ceremonies, and Customs

---

5519-PLAN-2060: Coordinate support for commitments

EVALUATION-CODED: NO   **SUSTAINMENT INTERVAL:** 6 months

BILLETS: Enlisted Conductor

GRADES: SSGT, GYSGT

INITIAL TRAINING SETTING: MOJT

CONDITION: Given an approved commitment for ceremonial musical support, letter of acceptance, administrative supplies, and commitment worksheet.

STANDARD: Ensuring the commitment worksheet is 100% accurate and all musical requirements are accomplished.

PERFORMANCE STEPS:
1. Review previous commitment after action reports when available.
2. Review commitment folder.
3. Contact sponsor.
4. Determine performance requirements.
5. Program music.
6. Determine performance area.
7. Confirm sequence of events with sponsor.
8. Coordinate logistical support.
9. Determine sound reinforcement requirements.
10. Determine set up requirements.
11. Task section leaders.
12. Determine required personnel for commitment.
13. Ensure TAD orders are generated, as required.
14. Plan rehearsal requirements.
15. Create program notes.

REFERENCES:
1. MCO 5726.15 Marine Corps Band Support of Community Relations
2. MCO P5000.18_ Marine Corps Band Manual
3. MCO P5060.20_ w/Ch 1 Marine Corps Drill and Ceremonies Manual
4. NAVSO P-6034 The Joint Federal Travel Regulations (JFTR), Volume 1

5519-TRNG-2080: Manage musician development

EVALUATION-CODED: NO   **SUSTAINMENT INTERVAL:** 12 months

BILLETS: Enlisted Conductor

GRADES: SSGT, GYSGT

INITIAL TRAINING SETTING: MOJT

CONDITION: Given Band personnel, audition book, and audition materials.

STANDARD: To create a systematic approach for development to meet technical proficiency requirements.

PERFORMANCE STEPS:
1. Observe musicians performing in ensemble.
2. Evaluate personnel as required.
3. Provide feedback on evaluations.
4. Identify goals for development of musical proficiency.
5. Create lesson plan.
6. Schedule future counseling.
7. Supervise execution of lesson plan tasks.

REFERENCES:
1. MCO P5000.18_ Marine Corps Band Manual
2. MUSCOLINST 1300.1 Audition Standards Manual

MUSIC T&R MANUAL

CHAPTER 6

MOS 5521 INDIVIDUAL EVENTS

MUSIC T&R MANUAL

CHAPTER 6

MOS 5521 INDIVIDUAL EVENTS

6000. PURPOSE. This chapter details the individual events that pertain to the occupational field 55, Music. These events are linked to a service-level Mission Essential Tasks (MET). This linkage tailors individual training for the selected MET. Each individual event provides an event title, along with the conditions events will be performed under, and the standard to which the event must be performed to be successful.

6001. ADMINISTRATIVE NOTES. T&R events are coded for ease of reference. T&R events are coded for ease of reference. Events in the T&R Manual are depicted with a 12 field alphanumeric system, i.e. 5521-BNDR-2010. This chapter utilizes the following methodology:

a. The first four digits represent the occupational field or military occupational field (e.g., Occupational Field 55 or Drum Major MOS 5521). This chapter contains 5521 events.

b. The second four alpha characters represent the functional or duty area (e.g., PERF – Performance). The functional areas for Drum Majors are:

    ADMN – Administration
    AUDN – Audition
    FDRL – Field Drill
    CREL – Community Relations
    PLAN – Planning
    TRNG – Training

c. The last four digits represent the task level and numerical sequencing. The Music individual training events are separated into two task levels:

    1000 – Core Skills (initial MOS training conducted at formal schools)
    2000 – Core Plus Skills (follow-on formal schooling, MOJT or distance
           learning)

Every individual event has a numerical identifier from 001 to 999.

d. The individual task condition statement sets forth the real-world circumstances in which the task is to be performed. Condition statements describe the equipment, tools, materials, environmental or safety considerations, and resources need to perform the task and the assistance, location, etc. that relates to performance of the task. In a garrison or field environment and with the aid of references are common conditions for all Occupational Field 55 tasks unless otherwise noted.

6002. INDEX OF INDIVIDUAL EVENTS

1. **2000-LEVEL EVENTS.** There are no 1000-level individual events for Drum Majors. 2000-level individual events for Drum Majors are taught at either follow-on schools, by MOJT or through Distance Learning.

EVENT	DESCRIPTION	PAGE
	ADMINISTRATION	
5521-ADMN-2001	Manage assigned logistical areas	6-4
	AUDITION	
5521-AUDN-2010	Audition personnel	6-4
	COMMUNITY RELATIONS	
5521-CREL-2020	Deliver Marine Corps Band marketing presentation	6-5
	FIELD DRILL	
5521-FDLR-2030	Lead field drill	6-5
	PLANNING	
5521-PLAN-2060	Coordinate support for commitments	6-6
	TRAINING	
5521-TRNG-2080	Manage musician development	6-6

6003. 2000-LEVEL EVENTS

5521-ADMN-2001: Manage assigned logistical areas

EVALUATION-CODED: NO   **SUSTAINMENT INTERVAL:** 12 months

BILLETS: Drum Major

GRADES: SSGT, GYSGT

INITIAL TRAINING SETTING: MOJT

CONDITION: Given band personnel.

STANDARD: Ensure all assigned areas remain 100% mission capable.

PERFORMANCE STEPS:
1. Manage Admin Section.
2. Manage Loading Section
3. Manage Transportation Section.
4. Train assigned personnel.

REFERENCE:
1. MCO P5000.18_ Marine Corps Band Manual

5521-AUDN-2010: Audition personnel

EVALUATION-CODED: NO   **SUSTAINMENT INTERVAL:** 6 Months

BILLETS: Drum Major

GRADES: SSGT, GYSGT

INITIAL TRAINING SETTING: FORMAL

CONDITION: Given an instrumentalist with instrument, music stand, audition book, administrative materials, copy of auditionee's solo, metronome, and designated location.

STANDARD: In performance step sequence, to ascertain technical proficiency and ensuring 98% accuracy and consistency with the Audition Standards Manual.

PERFORMANCE STEPS:
1. Grade prepared material.
2. Grade performance of rudiments or scales.
3. Grade performance of sight reading material.
4. Average numerical score for all criteria.
5. Evaluate memorized music as required.

REFERENCES:
1. MCO P5000.18_ Marine Corps Band Manual
2. MUSCOLINST 1300.1 Audition Standards Manual

5521-CREL-2020: Deliver Marine Corps Band marketing presentation

EVALUATION-CODED: NO   **SUSTAINMENT INTERVAL**: 12 months

BILLETS: Drum Major

GRADES: SSGT, GYSGT

INITIAL TRAINING SETTING: FORMAL

CONDITION: Given a targeted audience, current band information, and computer with presentation software.

STANDARD: Clearly and concisely address current leadership and performance opportunities within Marine Corps Bands.

PERFORMANCE STEPS:
1. Schedule presentation.
2. Gather demographic information on civilian musical unit.
3. Prepare presentation outline.
4. Rehearse presentation outline.
5. Deliver presentation.
6. Answer questions.
7. Provide feedback to Marine Corps Recruiting Command.

REFERENCES:
1. MCO 1130.53P w/Ch 1 Enlistment Incentive Programs
2. MCO 5726.15 Marine Corps Band Support of Community Relations
3. MCO P5000.18_ Marine Corps Band Manual
4. MCRC VOLUME 3-Guidebook for Recruiting Station Operations

5521-FDRL-2030: Lead field drill

EVALUATION-CODED: NO   **SUSTAINMENT INTERVAL**: 12 months

BILLETS: Drum Major

GRADES: SSGT, GYSGT

INITIAL TRAINING SETTING: FORMAL

CONDITION: Given a mace, a fully equipped band, and marching area.

STANDARD: Performing and rehearsing at a 3.0 level.

PERFORMANCE STEPS:
1. Brief the sequence of events to the Band.
2. Dictate maneuver using verbal commands or mace signals, as appropriate.
3. Correct music and drill, as appropriate.
4. Execute sequence of events.
5. Program appropriate music.

REFERENCES:
1. MCO P5000.18B Marine Corps Band Manual
2. MCO P5060.20_ Marine Corps Drill and Ceremonies Manual
3. U.S. Navy Regulations Chapter 12 - Flags, Pennants, Honors, Ceremonies, and Customs

---

5521-PLAN-2060: Coordinate support for commitments

EVALUATION-CODED: NO   **SUSTAINMENT INTERVAL:** 12 months

BILLETS: Drum Major

GRADES: SSGT, GYSGT

INITIAL TRAINING SETTING: MOJT

CONDITION: Given an approved commitment for ceremonial musical support, letter of acceptance, administrative supplies, and commitment worksheet.

STANDARD: Ensuring the commitment worksheet is 100% accurate and all musical requirements are accomplished.

PERFORMANCE STEPS:
1. Review previous commitment after action reports when available.
2. Review commitment folder.
3. Contact sponsor.
4. Determine performance requirements.
5. Program music.
6. Determine performance area.
7. Confirm sequence of events with sponsor.
8. Coordinate logistical support.
9. Determine sound reinforcement requirements.
10. Determine set up requirements.
11. Task section leaders.
12. Determine required personnel for commitment.
13. Ensure TAD orders are generated, as required.
14. Plan rehearsal requirements.

REFERENCES:
1. MCO 5726.15 Marine Corps Band Support of Community Relations
2. MCO P5000.18_ Marine Corps Band Manual
3. MCO P5060.20_ w/Ch 1 Marine Corps Drill and Ceremonies Manual
4. NAVSO P-6034 The Joint Federal Travel Regulations (JFTR), Volume 1

5521-TRNG-2080: Manage musician development

EVALUATION-CODED: NO   **SUSTAINMENT INTERVAL:** 12 months

BILLETS: Drum Major

GRADES: SSGT, GYSGT

INITIAL TRAINING SETTING: MOJT

CONDITION: Given band personnel.

STANDARD: To create a systematic approach for development to meet technical proficiency requirements.

PERFORMANCE STEPS:
1. Observe musicians performing in ensemble.
2. Evaluate personnel as required.
3. Provide feedback on evaluations.
4. Identify goals for development of proficiency.
5. Create Lesson Plan.
6. Schedule future counseling.
7. Supervise execution of lesson plan tasks.

REFERENCES:
1. MCO P5000.18_ Marine Corps Band Manual
2. MUSCOLINST 1300.1 Audition Standards Manual

MUSIC T&R MANUAL

CHAPTER 7

MOS 5522 INDIVIDUAL EVENTS

CHAPTER 7

MOS 5522 INDIVIDUAL EVENTS

7000. PURPOSE. This chapter details the individual events that pertain to the occupational field 55, Music. These events are linked to a service-level Mission Essential Tasks (MET). This linkage tailors individual training for the selected MET. Each individual event provides an event title, along with the conditions events will be performed under, and the standard to which the event must be performed to be successful.

7001. ADMINISTRATIVE NOTES. T&R events are coded for ease of reference. Events in the T&R Manual are depicted with a 12 field alphanumeric system, i.e. 5522-PERF-1075. This chapter utilizes the following methodology:

a. The first four digits represent the occupational field or military occupational field (e.g., Occupational Field 55 or Small Ensemble Leader MOS 5522). This chapter contains 5522 events.

b. The second four alpha characters represent the functional or duty area (e.g., ADMN - Administration). Functional areas for Small Ensemble Leaders are:

    ADMN - Administration
    AUDN - Audition
    PERF - Performance
    PLAN - Planning
    TRNG - Training

c. The last four digits represent the task level and numerical sequencing. The Music individual training events are separated into two task levels:

    1000 - Core Skills (initial MOS training conducted at formal schools)
    2000 - Core Plus Skills (follow-on formal schooling, MOJT or distance
           learning)

Every individual event has a numerical identifier from 001 to 999.

d. The individual task condition statement sets forth the real-world circumstances in which the task is to be performed. Condition statements describe the equipment, tools, materials, environmental or safety considerations, and resources need to perform the task and the assistance, location, etc. that relates to performance of the task. In a garrison or field environment and with the aid of references are common conditions for all Occupational Field 55 tasks unless otherwise noted.

7002. INDEX OF INDIVIDUAL EVENTS

1. **2000-LEVEL EVENTS.** 2000-level individual events for Small Ensemble Leaders are taught at either follow-on schools, by MOJT or through Distance Learning.

EVENT	DESCRIPTION	PAGE
	ADMINISTRATION	
5522-ADMN-2001	Manage assigned logistical areas	7-4
	AUDITION	
5522-AUDN-2010	Audition personnel	7-4
	PEFFORMANCE	
5522-PERF-2050	Lead small ensembles	7-5
5522-PERF-2051	Perform music in an ensemble	7-5
5522-PERF-2052	Perform assigned instrument	7-6
	PLANNING	
5522-PLAN-2060	Coordinate support for commitments	7-6
	TRAINING	
5522-TRNG-2080	Manage musician development	7-7

7003. 2000-LEVEL EVENTS

5522-ADMN-2001: Manage assigned logistical areas

EVALUATION-CODED: NO   **SUSTAINMENT INTERVAL**: 12 months

BILLETS: Small Ensemble Leader

GRADES: SSGT, GYSGT

INITIAL TRAINING SETTING: MOJT

CONDITION: Given Band personnel.

STANDARD: Ensure all assigned areas remain 100% mission capable.

PERFORMANCE STEPS:
1. Oversee Audio/Visual Section.
2. Train assigned personnel

REFERENCE:
1. MCO P5000.18_ Marine Corps Band Manual

5522-AUDN-2010: Audition personnel

EVALUATION-CODED: NO   **SUSTAINMENT INTERVAL**: 6 months

BILLETS: Small Ensemble Leader

GRADES: SSGT, GYSGT

INITIAL TRAINING SETTING: FORMAL

CONDITION: Given an instrumentalist with instrument, music stand, audition book, administrative materials, copy of auditionee's solo, metronome, and designated location.

STANDARD: In performance step sequence, to ascertain technical proficiency and ensuring 98% accuracy and consistency with the Audition Standards Manual.

PERFORMANCE STEPS:
1. Grade prepared material.
2. Grade performance of rudiments or scales.
3. Grade performance of sight reading material.
4. Average numerical score for all criteria.
5. Evaluate memorized music as required.

REFERENCES:
1. MCO P5000.18_ Marine Corps Band Manual
2. MUSCOLINST 1300.1 Audition Standards Manual

5522-PERF-2050: Lead small ensembles

EVALUATION-CODED: NO   **SUSTAINMENT INTERVAL**: 12 months

BILLETS: Small Ensemble Leader

GRADES: SSGT, GYSGT

INITIAL TRAINING SETTING: FORMAL

DESCRIPTION: Required small ensembles are defined in the MCO P5000.18_.

CONDITION: Given a fully equipped ensemble and a performance venue.

STANDARD: Directing and rehearsing all small ensembles at a 3.0 level.

PERFORMANCE STEPS:
1. Brief the sequence of events to ensemble.
2. Direct ensemble using proper techniques.
3. Correct music in rehearsal as appropriate.
4. Execute sequence of events.
5. Program appropriate music.

REFERENCE:
1. MCO P5000.18_ Marine Corps Band Manual
2. MCO P5060.20_ Marine Corps Drill and Ceremonies Manual
3. U. S. Navy Regulations w/Ch 1 Chapter 12 - Flags, Pennants, Honors, Ceremonies, and Customs

---

5522-PERF-2051: Perform music in an ensemble

EVALUATION-CODED: NO   **SUSTAINMENT INTERVAL**: 12 months

BILLETS: Small Ensemble Leader

GRADES: SSGT, GYSGT

INITIAL TRAINING SETTING: FORMAL

DESCRIPTION: Ensembles include Concert Band, Ceremonial Band, Field Drill, Jazz Ensemble, Show Band, Combo, Party Band, Brass Quintet, and Woodwind Quintet.

CONDITION: As a member of a performing ensemble, given an assembled instrument, appropriate music, and a conductor or ensemble leader.

STANDARD: In accordance with the conductor's direction, ensuring notes, rhythm, and musicality are accurately produced to the appropriate instrument to a 3.0 level.

PERFORMANCE STEPS:
1. Properly tune instrument to a given pitch.
2. Perform the music, following the conductor's direction.

3. Make individual adjustments, as necessary, to provide proper balance
within the ensemble.

REFERENCE:
1. MCO P5000.18_ Marine Corps Band Manual

5522-PERF-2052: Perform assigned instrument

EVALUATION-CODED: NO   **SUSTAINMENT INTERVAL:** 12 months

BILLETS: Small Ensemble Leader

GRADES: SSGT, GYSGT

INITIAL TRAINING SETTING: FORMAL

CONDITION: Given an assembled instrument, an evaluator, designated location,
and prepared grade V solo.

STANDARD: At a 3.0 level.

PERFORMANCE STEPS:
1. Perform prepared piece.
2. Perform scales or rudiments designated by the evaluator.
3. Sight read music as provided by the evaluator.
4. Perform memorized music as required.

REFERENCES:
1. MCO P5000.18_ Marine Corps Band Manual
2. MUSCOLINST 1300.1_ Audition Standards Manual

5522-PLAN-2060: Coordinate support for commitments

EVALUATION-CODED: NO   **SUSTAINMENT INTERVAL:** 12 Months

BILLETS: Small Ensemble Leader

GRADES: SSGT, GYSGT

INITIAL TRAINING SETTING: MOJT

CONDITION: Given an approved commitment for small ensemble support, letter
of acceptance, administrative supplies, and commitment worksheet.

STANDARD: Ensuring the commitment worksheet is 100% accurate and all musical
requirements are accomplished.

PERFORMANCE STEPS:
1. Review previous commitment after action reports when available.
2. Review commitment folder.
3. Contact sponsor.

4. Determine performance requirements.
5. Program music.
6. Determine performance area.
7. Confirm sequence of events with sponsor.
8. Coordinate logistical support.
9. Determine sound reinforcement requirements.
10. Determine set up requirements.
11. Task ensemble leaders.
12. Determine required personnel for commitment.
13. Ensure TAD orders are generated, as required.
14. Plan rehearsal requirements.
15. Create program notes.

REFERENCES:
1. MCO 5726.15 Marine Corps Band Support of Community Relations
2. MCO P5000.18_ Marine Corps Band Manual
3. MCO P5060.20_ w/Ch 1 Marine Corps Drill and Ceremonies Manual
4. NAVSO P-6034 The Joint Federal Travel Regulations (JFTR), Volume 1

5522-TRNG-2080: Manage musician development

EVALUATION-CODED: NO   **SUSTAINMENT INTERVAL:** 12 months

BILLETS: Small Ensemble Leader

GRADES: SSGT, GYSGT

INITIAL TRAINING SETTING: MOJT

CONDITION: Given Band personnel, audition book, and audition materials.

STANDARD: To create a systematic approach for development to meet technical proficiency requirements.

PERFORMANCE STEPS:
1. Observe musicians performing in ensemble.
2. Evaluate personnel as required.
3. Provide feedback on evaluations.
4. Identify goals for development of musical proficiency.
5. Create lesson plan.
6. Schedule future counseling.
7. Supervise execution of lesson plan tasks.

REFERENCES:
1. MCO P5000.18_ Marine Corps Band Manual
2. MUSCOLINST 1300.1 Audition Standards Manual

NAVMC 3500.28A
15 Feb 2011

MUSIC T&R MANUAL

CHAPTER 8

MOS 5523 INDIVIDUAL EVENTS

MUSIC T&R MANUAL

CHAPTER 8

MOS 5523 INDIVIDUAL EVENTS

8000. PURPOSE. This chapter details the individual events that pertain to the occupational field 55, Music. These events are linked to a service-level Mission Essential Tasks (MET). This linkage tailors individual training for the selected MET. Each individual event provides an event title, along with the conditions events will be performed under, and the standard to which the event must be performed to be successful.

8001. ADMINISTRATIVE NOTES. T&R events are coded for ease of reference. T&R events are coded for ease of reference. Events in the T&R Manual are depicted with a 12 field alphanumeric system, i.e. 5523-HZMG-2040. This chapter utilizes the following methodology:

a. The first four digits represent the occupational field or military occupational field (e.g., Occupational Field 55 or Instrument Repair Technician MOS 5523). This chapter contains 5523 events.

b. The second four alpha characters represent the functional or duty area (e.g., ADMN – Administration). The functional areas for Instrument Repair Technicians are:

    ADMN - Administration
    FISC - Fiscal
    HZMG - Hazardous Material Management
    MANT - Maintenance
    PLAN - Planning
    SAFE - Safety
    SUPT - Support

c. The last four digits represent the task level and numerical sequencing. The Music individual training events are separated into two task levels:

    1000 – Core Skills (initial MOS training conducted at formal schools)
    2000 – Core Plus Skills (follow-on formal schooling, MOJT or distance learning)

Every individual event has a numerical identifier from 001 to 999.

d. The individual task condition statement sets forth the real-world circumstances in which the task is to be performed. Condition statements describe the equipment, tools, materials, environmental or safety considerations, and resources need to perform the task and the assistance, location, etc. that relates to performance of the task. In a garrison or field environment and with the aid of references are common conditions for all Occupational Field 55 tasks unless otherwise noted.

8002. INDEX OF INDIVIDUAL EVENTS

1. **2000-LEVEL EVENTS.** There are no 1000-level individual events for Instrument Repair Technicians. 2000-level individual events for Instrument Repair Technicians are taught at either follow-on schools, by MOJT or through Distance Learning.

EVENT	DESCRIPTION	PAGE
	ADMINISTRATION	
5523-ADMN-2001	Maintain building maintenance log	8-4
5523-ADMN-2002	Maintain instrument history logbook	8-4
	FISCAL	
5523-FISC-2040	Develop annual budget	8-5
5523-FISC-2041	Develop Periodic Replacement Plan (PRP)	8-5
	HAZARDOUS MATRIAL MANAGEMENT	
5523-HZMG-2050	Maintain hazardous material (HAZMAT) program	8-6
	MAINTENANCE	
5523-MANT-2060	Maintain instrument repair tools/equipment	8-6
5523-MANT-2061	Inspect all band instruments	8-7
5523-MANT-2062	Perform maintenance on instruments	8-8
5523-MANT-2063	Evaluate requirement for 5th echelon maintenance	8-8
	PLANNING	
5523-PLAN-2070	Manage unit embarkation plan	8-9
	SAFETY	
5523-SAFE-2080	Manage Band safety program	8-9
5523-SAFE-2081	Manage Band hearing conservation program	8-10
	SUPPORT	
5523-SUPT-2090	Supervise Supply Section	8-11
5523-SUPT-2091	Manage procurement of musical instruments, supplies, and equipment	8-11
5523-SUPT-2092	Inventory serialized Band equipment	8-12
5523-SUPT-2093	Inventory instrument repair supplies	8-12
5523-SUPT-2094	Supervise disposal of unserviceable Band instruments/equipment	8-13

8003. 2000-LEVEL EVENTS

5523-ADMN-2001: Maintain building maintenance log

EVALUATION-CODED: NO   **SUSTAINMENT INTERVAL**: 12 months

BILLETS: Instrument Repair Technician

GRADES: SSGT, GYSGT, MSGT, MGYSGT

INITIAL TRAINING SETTING: MOJT

CONDITION: Given maintenance personnel, facility, building maintenance log, and administrative supplies.

STANDARD: To ensure building maintenance is tracked with 100% accuracy and currency.

PERFORMANCE STEPS:
1. Inspect building for maintenance problems.
2. Identify discrepancies.
3. Complete minor repairs as authorized.
4. Contact facilities maintenance for all other repairs.
6. Update maintenance log as required.

REFERENCE:
1. MCO P5000.18B Marine Corps Band Manual

5523-ADMN-2002: Maintain instrument history logbook

EVALUATION-CODED: NO   **SUSTAINMENT INTERVAL**: 12 months

BILLETS: Instrument Repair Technician

GRADES: SSGT, GYSGT, MSGT, MGYSGT

INITIAL TRAINING SETTING: MOJT

CONDITION: Given repair personnel, instrument requisitions, and repair records.

STANDARD: To ensure 100% accuracy and currency of instrument history.

PERFORMANCE STEPS:
1. Generate an individual historical record for each instrument.
2. Record all instrument repairs in individual records.

REFERENCE:
1. MCO P5000.18B Marine Corps Band Manual

5523-FISC-2040: Develop annual budget

EVALUATION-CODED: NO   **SUSTAINMENT INTERVAL**: 12 months

BILLETS: Instrument Repair Technician

GRADES: SSGT, GYSGT, MSGT, MGYSGT

INITIAL TRAINING SETTING: MOJT

CONDITION: Given command budget guidance, historical budget records, the Periodic Replacement Plan (PRP), immediate equipment requirements, and section input.

STANDARD: Ensuring all funding requirements and deficiencies are identified with 100% accuracy.

PERFORMANCE STEPS:
1. Review historical budget records.
2. Determine annual budget requirements.
3. Submit draft budget to Band Officer for approval.
4. Execute annual budget plan.

REFERENCES:
1. MCO 4400.163 DoD Supply Management Reference Book
2. MCO P4400.150E W/ERRATUM CH 1-2 Consumer Level Policy Manual
3. MCO P5000.18B Marine Corps Band Manual
4. MCO P7100.8K Field Budget Guidance Manual

5523-FISC-2041: Develop Periodic Replacement Plan (PRP)

EVALUATION-CODED: NO   **SUSTAINMENT INTERVAL**: 12 months

BILLETS: Instrument Repair Technician

GRADES: SSGT, GYSGT, MSGT, MGYSGT

INITIAL TRAINING SETTING: MOJT

CONDITION: Given the Table of Organization and Equipment (TO&E) and current Consolidate Memorandum of Receipt (CMR).

STANDARD: To ensure all TO&E requirements are properly identified and adjusted to meet budget constraints.

PERFORMANCE STEPS:
1. Review current CMR for equipment accountability.
2. Determine history and age of each piece of equipment.
3. Determine proper replacement year for each musical instrument within the PRP, using a 7-year replacement cycle.
4. Determine proper replacement year for each piece of electronic gear within the PRP using 3-year replacement cycle.

REFERENCE:
1. MCO P5000.18_ Marine Corps Band Manual

5523-HZMG-2050: Manage hazardous material (HAZMAT) program

EVALUATION-CODED: NO   **SUSTAINMENT INTERVAL:** 12 months

BILLETS: Instrument Repair Technician

GRADES: SSGT, GYSGT, MSGT, MGYSGT

INITIAL TRAINING SETTING: FORMAL

CONDITION: Given facilities, hazardous material, the command HAZMAT program, administrative supplies, and a computer with software.

STANDARD: To ensure establishment of required HAZMAT procedures.

PERFORMANCE STEPS:
1. Review command HAZMAT program.
2. Publish unit HAZMAT program.
3. Identify personnel for HAZMAT training.
4. Submit appropriate documents for authorization and procurement.
5. Inventory all hazardous material.
6. Maintain Material Safety Data Sheet (MSDS) book for materials on hand.
7. Maintain spill containment kit.
8. Schedule removal of HAZMAT.

REFERENCES:
1. MCO 4450.12A Storage and Handling of Hazardous Materials
2. MCO 5100.8 Marine Corps Occupational Safety and Health (OSH) Policy Order
3. MCO P5090.2A Environmental Compliance and Protection Manual
4. UFC 4-171-04AN Department of Defense Design Guide - Band Training Facilities

SUPPORT REQUIREMENTS:

Other/Miscellaneous: Coordinate assistance from installation/Base Environmental Office, Safety Office per MCO 5100.8_ and MCO P5090.2_.

5523-MANT-2060: Maintain instrument repair tools/equipment

EVALUATION-CODED: NO   **SUSTAINMENT INTERVAL:** 12 months

BILLETS: Instrument Repair Technician

GRADES: SSGT, GYSGT, MSGT, MGYSGT

INITIAL TRAINING SETTING: FORMAL

CONDITION: Given repair personnel, repair tools/equipment, and cleaning and maintenance supplies.

STANDARD: To ensure 100% serviceability.

PERFORMANCE STEPS:
1. Inventory tools/equipment.
2. Inspect tools/equipment for serviceability.
3. Restore to serviceable condition.
4. Apply a light coat of rust inhibitor on tools/equipment.
5. Update records.

REFERENCES:
1. BECKWITH, GENE E.; HUTH, JOHN BAND INSTRUMENT REPAIR MANUAL; Minnesota SE Technical College (2001)
2. KRAR, S. F. MACHINE TOOL OPERATIONS; Publisher: McGraw-Hill Inc. (1983)
3. MCO P5000.18_ Marine Corps Band Manual

5523-MANT-2061: Inspect all Band instruments

EVALUATION-CODED: NO   **SUSTAINMENT INTERVAL:** 12 months

BILLETS: Instrument Repair Technician

GRADES: SSGT, GYSGT, MSGT, MGYSGT

INITIAL TRAINING SETTING: FORMAL

CONDITION: Given repair personnel, instruments, cleaning supplies and equipment, adequate facilities, and the current Consolidated Memorandum of Receipt (CMR).

STANDARD: To ensure 100% serviceability and maintenance of all instruments.

PERFORMANCE STEPS:
1. Use current CMR to inspect all instruments and equipment for proper maintenance.
2. Use current CMR to inspect all instruments and equipment for serviceability.
3. Identify condition of all instruments and equipment.
4. Update inspection log.
5. Identify necessary repairs.
6. Take necessary corrective action, if required.

REFERENCES:
1. BECKWITH, GENE E.; HUTH, JOHN BAND INSTRUMENT REPAIR MANUAL; Minnesota SE Technical College (2001)
2. MCO P5000.18_ Marine Corps Band Manual

5523-MANT-2062: Perform maintenance on instruments

EVALUATION-CODED: NO   **SUSTAINMENT INTERVAL**: 12 months

BILLETS: Instrument Repair Technician

GRADES: SSGT, GYSGT, MSGT, MGYSGT

INITIAL TRAINING SETTING: FORMAL

DESCRIPTION: Instrument Repair Technicians are required to perform echelon 2 through 4 maintenance as defined in MCO P5000.18_.

CONDITION: Given repair personnel, malfunctioning instrument, repair tools and equipment, supplies and materials, and adequate facilities.

STANDARD: To return instrument to manufacturer standards.

PERFORMANCE STEPS:
1. Determine work required.
2. Perform required work.
3. Play test instrument.
4. Make necessary adjustments.
5. Update maintenance records.
6. Return to proper disposition.

REFERENCES:
1. BECKWITH, GENE E.; HUTH, JOHN BAND INSTRUMENT REPAIR MANUAL; Minnesota SE Technical College (2001)
2. BRAND, ERICK D. BAND INSTRUMENT REPAIRING MANUAL; Ferree's Tools Inc. (1993)
3. MCO P5000.18B Marine Corps Band Manual

5523-MANT-2063: Evaluate requirement for 5th echelon maintenance

EVALUATION-CODED: NO   **SUSTAINMENT INTERVAL**: 12 months

BILLETS: Instrument Repair Technician

GRADES: SSGT, GYSGT, MSGT, MGYSGT

INITIAL TRAINING SETTING: FORMAL

CONDITION: Given repair personnel, malfunctioning instrument/equipment, diagnostic equipment, and adequate facilities.

STANDARD: To identify all instruments and equipment requiring 5th echelon maintenance.

PERFORMANCE STEPS:
1. Diagnose malfunction.
2. Determine the level of work to be performed.
3. Identify qualified vendor to outsource repair.

4. Generate work requisition.
5. Deliver instrument/equipment for repair.
6. Update location records.
7. Receive instrument/equipment from vendor.
8. Inspect for serviceability.
9. Update maintenance and location records.
10. Return to proper disposition.

REFERENCES:
1. BECKWITH, GENE E.; HUTH, JOHN BAND INSTRUMENT REPAIR MANUAL; Minnesota SE Technical College (2001)
2. MCO P5000.18B Marine Corps Band Manual

5523-PLAN-2070: Manage unit embarkation plan

EVALUATION-CODED: NO   **SUSTAINMENT INTERVAL:** 12 months

BILLETS: Instrument Repair Technician

GRADES: SSGT, GYSGT, MSGT, MGYSGT

INITIAL TRAINING SETTING: MOJT

CONDITION: Given Command Embarkation Plan, Table of Organization and Equipment (TO&E), administrative supplies, computer, operational order.

STANDARD: In accordance with the command's embarkation plan.

PERFORMANCE STEPS:
1. Review command embarkation plan.
2. Develop unit embarkation plan.
3. Submit draft for review.
4. Correct deficiencies.
5. Publish unit embarkation plan.

REFERENCE:
1. MCO P5000.18_ Marine Corps Band Manual
2. Local SOP

5523-SAFE-2080: Manage Band safety program

EVALUATION-CODED: NO   **SUSTAINMENT INTERVAL:** 12 months

BILLETS: Instrument Repair Technician

GRADES: SSGT, GYSGT, MSGT, MGYSGT

INITIAL TRAINING SETTING: MOJT

CONDITION: Given administrative supplies, a computer, and the command safety program.

STANDARD: To ensure proper establishment of required safety procedures.

PERFORMANCE STEPS:
1. Review command safety program.
2. Conduct safety inspections.
3. Maintain appropriate safety program records.
4. Publish command safety program.

REFERENCES:
1. MCO 5100.29A W/Ch 1 Marine Corps Safety Program
2. Local SOP

SUPPORT REQUIREMENTS:
Other/Miscellaneous: Coordinate assistance from installation/Base Environmental Office, Safety Office, and supporting Medical Treatment Facility Industrial Hygiene Office per MCO 5100.8_ and MCO P5090.2_.

5523-SAFE-2081: Manage Band hearing conservation program

EVALUATION-CODED: NO   **SUSTAINMENT INTERVAL**: 12 months

BILLETS: Instrument Repair Technician

GRADES: SSGT, GYSGT, MSGT, MGYSGT

INITIAL TRAINING SETTING: MOJT

CONDITION: Given Band personnel.

STANDARD: To ensure the unit is in 100% compliance with MCO 6260.1_.

PERFORMANCE STEPS:
1. Schedule personnel for evaluation.
2. Ensure all personnel receive audiogram.
3. Ensure all personnel receive hearing protection device (HpD) fitting.
4. Ensure all personnel receive refresher training during annual medical evaluation.
5. Ensure all hazardous noise areas, work sites, and equipment are labeled.
6. Ensure all orders and directives are made available to personnel.
7. Maintain records.

REFERENCES:
1. 29 CFR 1910.95 Occupational Safety and Health Standards - Occupational noise exposure
2. MCO 6260.1E Marine Corps Hearing Conservation Program

SUPPORT REQUIREMENTS:
Other/Miscellaneous: Coordinate assistance from installation/Base Environmental Office, Safety Office, and supporting Medical Treatment Facility industrial hygiene office per MCO 5100.8_ and MCO P5090.2_.

5523-SUPT-2090: Supervise Supply Section

EVALUATION-CODED: NO   **SUSTAINMENT INTERVAL:** 12 months

BILLETS: Instrument Repair Technician

GRADES: SSGT, GYSGT, MSGT, MGYSGT

INITIAL TRAINING SETTING: MOJT

CONDITION: Given equipment and logistical requirements, supply personnel, and records.

STANDARD: To ensure the unit is 100% mission capable.

PERFORMANCE STEPS:
1. Train personnel to execute all required supply functions.
2. Verify accuracy of musical instrument inventory.
3. Verify accuracy of musical equipment inventory.
4. Verify accuracy of support equipment inventory.
5. Ensure musical instruments/equipment are properly maintained.

REFERENCES:
1. MCO 4340.1A w/Ch 1 Reporting Missing, Lost, Stolen, or Recovered (MLSR) Government Property
2. MCO 4400.163 DoD Supply Management Reference Book
3. MCO 4450.12A Storage and Handling of Hazardous Materials
4. MCO 4600.40A Government Travel Charge Card Program (GTCCP)
5. MCO 5100.29A w/Ch 1 Marine Corps Safety Program
6. MCO 5100.8 Marine Corps Occupational Safety and Health (OSH) Policy Order
7. MCO 6260.1E Marine Corps Hearing Conservation Program
8. MCO P4200.15 Marine Corps Purchasing Procedures Manual
9. MCO P4400.150E W/ERRATUM CH 1-2 Consumer Level Policy Manual
10. MCO P5000.18_ Marine Corps Band Manual
11. MCO P5090.2A Environmental Compliance and Protection Manual
12. MCO P5102.1_ Marine Corps Ground Mishap Reporting
13. MCO P7100.8K Field Budget Guidance Manual
14. OPNAVINST 4631.2 D Management of Department of the Navy (DON) Airlift Assets

---

5523-SUPT-2091: Manage procurement of musical instruments, supplies, and equipment

EVALUATION-CODED: NO   **SUSTAINMENT INTERVAL:** 12 months

BILLETS: Instrument Repair Technician

GRADES: SSGT, GYSGT, MSGT, MGYSGT

INITIAL TRAINING SETTING: MOJT

CONDITION: Given the Periodic Replacement Plan (PRP), annual budget, instruments/equipment supply sources, and Section input.

STANDARD: To meet all unit Table of Organization and Equipment (TO&E) requirements.

PERFORMANCE STEPS:
1. Identify instruments, supplies and equipment for purchase.
2. Research supply sources for cost and availability.
3. Forward purchase requests to Band Officer for approval.
4. Submit requisitions to appropriate authority.
5. Inspect receive instruments, supplies, and equipment.
6. Ensure new instrument, supplies and equipment are documented.

REFERENCES:
2. MCO P4200.15 Marine Corps Purchasing Procedures Manual
3. MCO P4400.150E W/ERRATUM CH 1-2 Consumer Level Policy Manual
4. MCO P5000.18B Marine Corps Band Manual

5523-SUPT-2092: Inventory serialized Band equipment

EVALUATION-CODED: NO   **SUSTAINMENT INTERVAL**: 3 months

BILLETS: Instrument Repair Technician

GRADES: SSGT, GYSGT, MSGT, MGYSGT

INITIAL TRAINING SETTING: MOJT

CONDITION: Given supply personnel, the current Consolidated Memorandum of Receipt (CMR), and Band equipment.

STANDARD: To reconcile on-hand items with the CMR notating any discrepancies.

PERFORMANCE STEPS:
1. Facilitate inventory.
2. Generate reports.
3. Submit draft reconciliation to Band Officer.
4. Update records.

REFERENCE:
1. MCO P5000.18_ Marine Corps Band Manual

5523-SUPT-2093: Inventory instrument repair supplies

EVALUATION-CODED: NO   **SUSTAINMENT INTERVAL**: 12 months

BILLETS: Instrument Repair Technician

GRADES: SSGT, GYSGT, MSGT, MGYSGT

INITIAL TRAINING SETTING: MOJT

CONDITION: Given repair personnel, repair supplies, a repair supplies inventory list, and reorder points.

STANDARD: To reconcile on-hand items with the repair supplies inventory list.

PERFORMANCE STEPS:
1. Inventory repair supplies.
2. Reorder, as necessary.
3. Update inventory records.

REFERENCE:
1. MCO P5000.18_ Marine Corps Band Manual

5523-SUPT-2094: Supervise disposal of unserviceable Band instruments/equipment

EVALUATION-CODED: NO   SUSTAINMENT INTERVAL: 12 months

BILLETS: Instrument Repair Technician

GRADES: SSGT, GYSGT, MSGT, MGYSGT

INITIAL TRAINING SETTING: MOJT

CONDITION: Given supply personnel, unserviceable band instruments/equipment, Defense Reutilization Management Office (DRMO) request form(s), and transportation.

STANDARD: To ensure proper disposal of all unserviceable Band instruments and equipment.

PERFORMANCE STEPS:
1. Identify unserviceable band instruments and equipment.
2. Complete DRMO request form.
3. Upon approval, submit completed DRMO request form.
4. Deliver instruments and equipment to DRMO facility.
5. Update records.

REFERENCES:
1. MCO P4400.150E W/ERRATUM Ch 1-2 Consumer Level Policy Manual
2. MCO P5000.18_Marine Corps Band Manual

MUSIC T&R MANUAL

CHAPTER 9

MOS 5524 INDIVIDUAL EVENTS

MUSIC T&R MANUAL

CHAPTER 9

MOS 5524 INDIVIDUAL EVENTS

9000. PURPOSE. This chapter details the individual events that pertain to the occupational field 55, Music. These events are linked to a service-level Mission Essential Tasks (MET). This linkage tailor's individual training for the selected MET. Each individual event provides an event title, along with the conditions events will be performed under, and the standard to which the event must be performed to be successful.

9001. ADMINISTRATIVE NOTES. T&R events are coded for ease of reference. Events in the T&R Manual are depicted with a 12 field alphanumeric system, i.e. 5524-BNDR-1011. This chapter utilizes the following methodology:

a. The first four digits represent the occupational field or military occupational field (e.g., Occupational Field 55 or Musician MOS 5524). This chapter contains 5524 events.

b. The second four alpha characters represent the functional or duty area (e.g., ADMN – Administration). Functional areas for Musicians are:

    ADMN – Administration
    AUDN – Audition
    FDRL – Field Drill
    CREL – Community Relations
    MANT – Maintenance
    PERF – Performance
    REHL – Rehearsal
    SUPT – Support

c. The last four digits represent the task level and numerical sequencing. The Music individual training events are separated into two task levels:

    1000 – Core Skills (initial MOS training conducted at formal schools)
    2000 – Core Plus Skills (follow-on formal schooling, MOJT or distance
           learning)

Every individual event has a numerical identifier from 001 to 999.

d. The individual task condition statement sets forth the real-world circumstances in which the task is to be performed. Condition statements describe the equipment, tools, materials, environmental or safety considerations, and resources need to perform the task and the assistance, location, etc. that relates to performance of the task. In a garrison or field environment and with the aid of references are common conditions for all Occupational Field 55 tasks unless otherwise noted.

9002. INDEX OF INDIVIDUAL EVENTS

1. 1000-LEVEL EVENTS

EVENT	DESCRIPTION	PAGE
	FIELD DRILL	
5524-FDRL-1030	Execute manual of the instrument	9-5
5524-FDRL-1031	Follow mace signals	9-5
	MAINTENANCE	
5524-MANT-1090	Perform 1st echelon maintenance on assigned woodwind instrument	9-6
5524-MANT-1091	Perform 1st echelon maintenance on assigned brass instrument	9-6
5524-MANT-1092	Perform 1st echelon maintenance on assigned percussion instrument	9-7
5524-MANT-1093	Produce reeds	9-7
	PERFORMANCE	
5524-PERF-1050	Perform assigned instrument to grade (2.7)	9-8
5524-PERF-1051	Perform assigned instrument to grade (2.8)	9-8
5524-PERF-1052	Perform assigned instrument to grade to grade (2.9)	9-9
5524-PERF-1053	Perform assigned instrument to grade (3.0)	9-9
5524-PERF-1054	Perform music in an ensemble	9-10
5524-PERF-1055	Perform pitched percussion instruments in an ensemble	9-10
5524-PERF-1056	Perform upright string bass in an ensemble	9-12

2. 2000-LEVEL EVENTS. Musician 2000-level individual events are taught at follow-on schools, by MOJT or through Distance Learning. Additionally, those Musicians that hold a section chief billet will develop and implement a local SOP for their subordinate logistical area(s). Section chiefs will also be responsible for the training of assigned personnel for their subordinate local area(s) as listed in their SOPs.

EVENT	DESCRIPTION	PAGE
	ADMINISTRATON	
5524-ADMN-2001	Write commitment After Action Report	9-12
5524-ADMN-2002	Maintain Band historical records	9-12
	AUDITION	
5524-AUDN-2010	Audition personnel	9-13
5524-AUDN-2011	Screen prospective applicant	9-13
5524-AUDN-2012	Audition prospective applicant	9-14
	COMMUNITY RELATIONS	
5524-CREL-2020	Coordinate publicity for performances	9-15
5524-CREL-2021	Design printed programs	9-15
5524-CREL-2022	Develop Band press package	9-16
5524-CREL-2023	Maintain websites	9-16
	FIELD DRILL	
5524-FDLR-2030	Lead field drill	9-17
	PERFORMANCE	
5524-PERF-2050	Lead Ceremonial Band	9-17

5524-PERF-2051	Write concert narration	9-18
5524-PERF-2052	Narrate concert	9-18
5524-PERF-2053	Improvise from lead sheet/chord changes	9-19
5524-PERF-2054	Lead small ensemble performance	9-19
5524-PERF-2055	Assemble audio/visual equipment	9-20
5524-PERF-2056	Operate audio/visual equipment	9-20
5524-SUPT-2057	Perform vocal music	9-21
	REHEARSAL	
5524-REHL-2060	Lead section rehearsal	9-21
	SUPPORT	
5524-SUPT-2070	Supervise Library Section	9-22
5524-SUPT-2071	Supervise Supply Section	9-23
5524-SUPT-2072	Inventory Band equipment	9-23
5524-SUPT-2073	Supervise Administrative Section	9-24
5524-SUPT-2074	Supervise Training Section	9-24
5524-SUPT-2075	Supervise Loading Section	9-25
5524-SUPT-2076	Supervise Transportation Section	9-25
5524-SUPT-2077	Supervise DTS Section	9-26

3. **2500-LEVEL EVENTS.** Musician 2500-level Master Sergeant through Master Gunnery Sergeant individual events are taught at follow-on schools, by MOJT or through Distance Learning. (Note: These 2500-level individual training events reflect the old MOS 5517 Bandmaster tasks.)

EVENT	DESCRIPTION	PAGE
	ADMINISTRATON	
5524-ADMN-2501	Supervise Band Intermediate Leadership	9-27
	AUDITION	
5524-AUDN-2510	Audition personnel	9-27
5524-AUDN-2511	Audition prospective applicant	9-28
	COMMUNITY RELATIONS	
5524-CREL-2520	Deliver Marine Corps band marketing presentation	9-28
	PLANNING	
5524-PLAN-2560	Develop annual operational plan	9-29
5524-PLAN-2561	Develop Band schedule	9-30
5524-PLAN-2562	Evaluate commitment requests	9-30

9003. 1000-LEVEL EVENTS

5524-FDRL-1030: Execute manual of the instrument

EVALUATION-CODED: NO   **SUSTAINMENT INTERVAL**: 12 months

BILLETS: Musician

GRADES: PVT, PFC, LCPL, CPL, SGT, SSGT, GYSGT

INITIAL TRAINING SETTING: FORMAL

DESCRIPTION: Oboe, bassoon, guitar, electric bass, and piano musicians will receive familiarity training in basic percussion and field drill techniques.

CONDITION: Given an assembled instrument and appropriate command and signal.

STANDARD: Demonstrating accurate placement of the instrument and body positions on the appropriate beat.

PERFORMANCE STEPS:
1. Review the reference for proper instrument manual.
2. Execute movements on the appropriate beat.

REFERENCE:
1. MCO P5000.18_ Marine Corps Band Manual

5524-FDRL-1031: Follow mace signals

EVALUATION-CODED: NO   **SUSTAINMENT INTERVAL**: 12 months

BILLETS: Musician

GRADES: PVT, PFC, LCPL, CPL, SGT, SSGT, GYSGT

INITIAL TRAINING SETTING: FORMAL

DESCRIPTION: Oboe, bassoon, guitar, electric bass and piano musicians will receive familiarity training in basic percussion and field drill techniques.

CONDITION: Given an assembled instrument and a Drum Major with mace.

STANDARD: Demonstrating proper instrument and body carriage in accordance with the Drum Major's commands.

PERFORMANCE STEPS:
1. Review the reference for appropriate instrument response to mace signals.
2. Assume position in formation.
3. Observe Drum Major's commands.
4. Execute movement/maneuver associated with the command.

REFERENCE:
1. MCO P5000.18_ Marine Corps Band Manual

5524-MANT-1090:   Perform 1st echelon maintenance on assigned woodwind instrument

EVALUATION-CODED: NO   **SUSTAINMENT INTERVAL:** 12 months

BILLETS: Musician

GRADES: PVT, PFC, LCPL, CPL, SGT, SSGT, GYSGT

INITIAL TRAINING SETTING: FORMAL

CONDITION: Given a woodwind instrument, instrument case, and cleaning equipment.

STANDARD: On a weekly basis, to ensure cleanliness, proper lubrication, and serviceability.

PERFORMANCE STEPS:
1. Disassemble the instrument.
2. Swab moisture from the inside of the bore.
3. Clean tone holes and keys.
4. Clean pads with a soft cloth.
5. Lubricate keys.
6. Clean instrument case.
7. Report any discrepancies to the Instrument Repair Technician.

REFERENCE:
1. MCO P5000.18_ Marine Corps Band Manual

5524-MANT-1091: Perform 1st echelon maintenance on assigned brass instrument

EVALUATION-CODED: NO   **SUSTAINMENT INTERVAL:** 12 months

BILLETS: Musician

GRADES: PVT, PFC, LCPL, CPL, SGT, SSGT, GYSGT

INITIAL TRAINING SETTING: FORMAL

CONDITION: Given a brass instrument, instrument case, and cleaning equipment.

STANDARD: On a weekly basis, to ensure cleanliness, proper lubrication, and serviceability.

PERFORMANCE STEPS:
1. Disassemble the instrument.
2. Submerge instrument and mouthpiece in lukewarm soapy water.

3. Scrub inside of brass instrument with snake or tubing brush.
4. Thoroughly dry instrument.
5. Lubricate valves and slides.
6. Polish the instrument.
7. Clean instrument case.
8. Report any discrepancies to the Instrument Repair Technician.

REFERENCE:
1. MCO P5000.18_ Marine Corps Band Manual

5524-MANT-1092: Perform 1st echelon maintenance on assigned percussion instrument

EVALUATION-CODED: NO   **SUSTAINMENT INTERVAL:** 12 months

BILLETS: Musician

GRADES: PVT, PFC, LCPL, CPL, SGT, SSGT, GYSGT

INITIAL TRAINING SETTING: FORMAL

CONDITION: Given a percussion instrument, instrument case, and cleaning equipment.

STANDARD: On a weekly basis, to ensure cleanliness and serviceability.

PERFORMANCE STEPS:
1. Tune drum heads, as appropriate.
2. Wipe down instrument with soft cloth.
3. Clean instrument case.
4. Report any discrepancies to the Instrument Repair Technician.

REFERENCE:
1. MCO P5000.18_ Marine Corps Band Manual

5524-MANT-1093: Produce reeds

EVALUATION-CODED: NO   **SUSTAINMENT INTERVAL:** 6 months

BILLETS: Musician Oboe and Bassoon

GRADES: PVT, PFC, LCPL, CPL, SGT, SSGT, GYSGT

INITIAL TRAINING SETTING: FORMAL

CONDITION: Given reed making materials and tools.

STANDARD: That meets industry standards.

PERFORMANCE STEPS:
1. Gather materials.
2. Assemble reeds.

REFERENCES:
1. The Oboe Reed Book, J. Light, 1983
2. Bassoon Reed Making: An Illustrated Method, Christopher Weait, 2008
3. Bassoon Reed Making, 3rd edition, Mark Popkin and Loren Glickman, 2007

5524-PERF-1050: Perform assigned instrument to grade

EVALUATION-CODED: NO　　　**SUSTAINMENT INTERVAL:** 6 months

BILLETS: Musician

GRADES: PVT, PFC, LCPL

INITIAL TRAINING SETTING: FORMAL

CONDITION: Given an assembled instrument, an evaluator, designated location, and prepared grade IV solo.

STANDARD: At a 2.7 level.

PERFORMANCE STEPS:
1. Perform prepared piece.
2. Perform scales or rudiments designated by the evaluator.
3. Sight read music as provided by the evaluator.
4. Perform memorized music as required.

REFERENCES:
1. MCO P5000.18_ Marine Corps Band Manual
2. MUSCOLINST 1300.1_ Audition Standards Manual

5524-PERF-1051: Perform assigned instrument to grade

EVALUATION-CODED: NO　　　**SUSTAINMENT INTERVAL:** 6 months

BILLETS: Musician

GRADES: CPL

INITIAL TRAINING SETTING: FORMAL

CONDITION: Given an assembled instrument, an evaluator, designated location, and prepared grade IV solo.

STANDARD: At a 2.8 level.

PERFORMANCE STEPS:
1. Perform prepared piece.

2. Perform scales or rudiments designated by the evaluator.
3. Sight read music as provided by the evaluator.
4. Perform memorized music as required.

REFERENCES:
1. MCO P5000.18_ Marine Corps Band Manual
2. MUSCOLINST 1300.1_ Audition Standards Manual

5524-PERF-1052: Perform assigned instrument to grade

EVALUATION-CODED: NO   **SUSTAINMENT INTERVAL:** 6 months

BILLETS: Musician

GRADES: SGT

INITIAL TRAINING SETTING: FORMAL

CONDITION: Given an assembled instrument, an evaluator, designated location, and prepared grade IV solo.

STANDARD: Pat a 2.9 level.

PERFORMANCE STEPS:
1. Perform prepared piece.
2. Perform scales or rudiments designated by the evaluator.
3. Sight read music as provided by the evaluator.
4. Perform memorized music as required.

REFERENCES:
1. MCO P5000.18_ Marine Corps Band Manual
2. MUSCOLINST 1300.1 Audition Standards Manual

5524-PERF-1053: Perform assigned instrument to grade

EVALUATION-CODED: NO   **SUSTAINMENT INTERVAL:** 6 months

BILLETS: Musician

GRADES: SSGT, GYSGT

INITIAL TRAINING SETTING: FORMAL

CONDITION: Given an assembled instrument, an evaluator, designated location, and prepared grade V solo.

STANDARD: At a 3.0 level.

PERFORMANCE STEPS:
1. Perform prepared piece.
2. Perform scales or rudiments designated by the evaluator.

3. Sight read music as provided by the evaluator.
4. Perform memorized music as required.

REFERENCES:
1. MCO P5000.18_ Marine Corps Band Manual
2. MUSCOLINST 1300.1_ Audition Standards Manual

5524-PERF-1054: Perform music in an ensemble

EVALUATION-CODED: NO   **SUSTAINMENT INTERVAL:** 12 months

BILLETS: Musician

GRADES: PVT, PFC, LCPL, CPL, SGT, SSGT, GYSGT

INITIAL TRAINING SETTING: FORMAL

DESCRIPTION: Ensembles include, Concert Band, Ceremonial Band, Field Drill, Jazz Ensemble, Show Band, Combo, Party Band, Brass Quintet, and Woodwind Quintet.

CONDITION: As a member of a performing ensemble, given an assembled instrument, appropriate music, and a conductor or ensemble leader.

STANDARD: In accordance with the conductor's direction, ensuring notes, rhythm, and musicality are accurately produced to the appropriate instrument level for grade.

PERFORMANCE STEPS:
1. Properly tune instrument to a given pitch.
2. Perform the music, following the conductor's direction.
3. Make individual adjustments, as necessary, to provide proper balance within the ensemble.

REFERENCE:
1. MCO P5000.18_ Marine Corps Band Manual

5524-PERF-1055: Perform pitched percussion instruments in an ensemble

EVALUATION-CODED: NO   **SUSTAINMENT INTERVAL:** 12 months

BILLETS: Musician Percussion

GRADES: PVT, PFC, LCPL, CPL, SGT, SSGT, GYSGT

INITIAL TRAINING SETTING: FORMAL

DESCRIPTION: Pitch percussion instruments include mallet instruments and timpani.

CONDITION: As a member of a performing ensemble, given a pitch percussion instrument, appropriate music, and a conductor or ensemble leader.

STANDARD: In accordance with the conductor's direction, ensuring notes, rhythm, and musicality are accurately produced to the industry standard.

PERFORMANCE STEPS:
1. Properly tune instrument to a given pitch, as appropriate.
2. Perform the music, following the conductor's direction.
3. Make individual adjustments, as necessary, to provide proper balance within the ensemble.

REFERENCES
1. MCO P5000.18_ Marine Corps Band Manual

5524-PERF-1056: Perform upright string bass in an ensemble

EVALUATION-CODED: NO   SUSTAINMENT INTERVAL: 12 months

BILLETS: Musician Electric Bass

GRADES: PVT, PFC, LCPL, CPL, SGT, SSGT, GYSGT

INITIAL TRAINING SETTING: FORMAL

CONDITION: As a member of a performing ensemble, given an upright string bass, bow, appropriate music, and a conductor or ensemble leader.

STANDARD: In accordance with the conductor's direction, ensuring notes, rhythm, and musicality are accurately produced to the industry standard.

PERFORMANCE STEPS:
1. Properly tune instrument to a given pitch, as appropriate.
2. Perform the music, following the conductor's direction.
3. Make individual adjustments, as necessary, to provide proper balance within the ensemble.

REFERENCE:
1. MCO P5000.18_ Marine Corps Band Manual

9004. 2000-LEVEL EVENTS

5524-ADMN-2001: Write commitment After Action Report

EVALUATION-CODED: NO   **SUSTAINMENT INTERVAL**: 12 months

BILLETS:

GRADES: CPL, SGT, SSGT, GYSGT, MSGT, MGYSGT

INITIAL TRAINING SETTING: MOJT

CONDITION: Given a blank After Action Report form and commitment folder pertaining to a completed commitment.

STANDARD: Within seven days, ensuring the report is 100% accurate and complete.

PERFORMANCE STEPS:
1. Review personal notes pertaining to commitment.
2. Review commitment folder for additional information, as required.
3. Complete appropriate After Action Report form.
4. Submit completed After Action Report, with commitment folder, to Bandmaster.

REFERENCES:
1. MCO 5726.15 Marine Corps Band Support of Community Relations
2. MCO P5000.18_ Marine Corps Band Manual
3. SECNAVINST 5720.44_ Public Affairs Policy and Regulations

5524-ADMN-2002: Maintain Band historical records

EVALUATION-CODED: NO   **SUSTAINMENT INTERVAL**: 12 months

BILLETS: Musician

GRADES: CPL, SGT, SSGT, GYSGT

INITIAL TRAINING SETTING: MOJT

CONDITION: When assigned to Band marketing and public affairs, given photographs, articles, programs, other files pertaining to the Band, a computer with appropriate software, and administrative supplies.

STANDARD: Ensuring the chronological records are 100% accurate and complete.

PERFORMANCE STEPS:
1. Collect all applicable materials.
2. Consolidate materials into a chronological record.
3. Utilize appropriate storage for all historical materials.

REFERENCES:
1. MCO P5000.18_ Marine Corps Band Manual
2. MCO P5750.1G w/Ch 1 Manual for the Marine Corps Historical Program

---

5524-AUDN-2010: Audition personnel

EVALUATION-CODED: NO   SUSTAINMENT INTERVAL: 6 months

BILLETS: Musician

GRADES: SSGT, GYSGT

INITIAL TRAINING SETTING: MOJT

CONDITION: Given an instrumentalist with instrument, music stand, audition book, administrative materials, copy of auditionee's solo, metronome, and designated location.

STANDARD: In performance step sequence, to ascertain technical proficiency and ensuring 95% accuracy and consistency with the Audition Standards Manual.

PERFORMANCE STEPS:
1. Grade prepared material.
2. Grade performance of rudiments or scales.
3. Grade performance of sight reading material.
4. Average numerical score for all criteria.
5. Evaluate memorized music as required.

REFERENCES:
1. MCO P5000.18_ Marine Corps Band Manual
2. MUSCOLINST 1300.1 Audition Standards Manual

5524-AUDN-2011: Screen prospective applicant

EVALUATION-CODED: NO   SUSTAINMENT INTERVAL: 6 months

BILLETS: Musician Technical Assistant

GRADES: SSGT, GYSGT, MSGT

INITIAL TRAINING SETTING: FORMAL

CONDITION: Given a prospective Marine musician applicant, administrative materials, a MEOP screening form, and designated location.

STANDARD: In performance step sequence, to properly evaluate the potential to pass an entry level instrumental audition.

PERFORMANCE STEPS:
1. Establish rapport with applicant.
2. Screen applicant for musical background.

3. Record results on screening form.
4. Determine applicant's audition eligibility.
5. Counsel applicant on eligibility determination.
6. If ineligible, counsel applicant on other options.
7. Schedule audition for eligible applicant.
8. Explain audition process to applicant.
9. Prepare applicant for audition.

REFERENCES:
1. MCO P5000.18_ Marine Corps Band Manual
2. MUSCOLINST 1300.1 Audition Standards Manual
3. MCBUL 1200 Military Occupational Specialties Manual
4. Marine Corps Opportunities Book

5524-AUDN-2012: Audition prospective applicant

EVALUATION-CODED: NO   **SUSTAINMENT INTERVAL:** 6 months

BILLETS: Musician Technical Assistant

GRADES: SSGT, GYSGT, MSGT

INITIAL TRAINING SETTING: FORMAL

CONDITION: Given a prospective Marine musician applicant with instrument, music stand, audition book, administrative materials, an audition form, a MEOP screening form, copy of auditionee's solo, metronome, designated location, and in a garrison environment.

STANDARD: In performance step sequence, to ascertain technical proficiency and ensuring 98% accuracy and consistency with the Audition Standards Manual.

PERFORMANCE STEPS:
1. Establish rapport with applicant.
2. Establish proper audition environment.
3. Determine if prepared solo meets required difficulty level.
4. Review auditions process with applicant.
5. Provide warm-up opportunity, if required.
6. Evaluate auditionee's competency by observing musical criteria demonstrated.
7. Describe each criterion observed in descriptive adjectives criteria form.
8. Record numerical score for each criterion that most accurately corresponds to descriptive adjective.
9. Average numerical score for all criteria.
10. Record final average in appropriate block on audition form.
11. Counsel auditionee on final results.
12. File copy of audition form.
13. Forward results, as required.

REFERENCES:
1. MCO P5000.18_ Marine Corps Band Manual
2. MUSCOLINST 1300.1 Audition Standards Manual
3. MCBUL 1200 Military Occupational Specialties Manual

5524-CREL-2020: Coordinate publicity for performances

EVALUATION-CODED: NO   **SUSTAINMENT INTERVAL**: 12 months

BILLETS: Public Affairs Chief

GRADES: SSGT, GYSGT

INITIAL TRAINING SETTING: MOJT

CONDITION: Given the type of ensemble, commitment date and time, location of performance, and access to local media.

STANDARD: To ensure community awareness by providing accurate and timely information of unit's operations to all applicable media contacts, in order to maximize attendance at public performances.

PERFORMANCE STEPS:
1. Determine suitable time frame to distribute pertinent information.
2. Coordinate with local civilian and military assets for the proper distribution of information.
3. Schedule interviews with media as available.
4. Follow up with contacts as necessary.
5. Ensure quality control of external media.

REFERENCES:
1. MCO 5726.15 Marine Corps Band Support of Community Relations
2. MCO P5000.18_ Marine Corps Band Manual
3. SECNAVINST 5720.44_ Public Affairs Policy and Regulations
4. StratCom - Strategic Communication Plan PCN 50100654400, dated July 2007

5524-CREL-2021: Design printed programs

EVALUATION-CODED: NO   **SUSTAINMENT INTERVAL**: 12 months

BILLETS: Marketing and Public Affairs Chief

GRADES: SGT, SSGT, GYSGT

INITIAL TRAINING SETTING: MOJT

CONDITION: Given a computer with appropriate software and information related to the performance.

STANDARD: Ensuring the printed programs contains all required information and are prepared with 100% accuracy.

PERFORMANCE STEPS:
1. Review all commitment information.
2. Coordinate information gathered into a cohesive program.
3. Review draft program for accuracy and artistic merit.
4. Upon approval, print suitable number of programs.

REFERENCES:
1. MCO 5726.15 Marine Corps Band Support of Community Relations
2. MCO P5000.18_ Marine Corps Band Manual

5524-CREL-2022: Develop Band press package

EVALUATION-CODED: NO   **SUSTAINMENT INTERVAL:** 12 months

BILLETS: Marketing and Public Affairs Chief

GRADES: SGT, SSGT, GYSGT

INITIAL TRAINING SETTING: MOJT

CONDITION: Given a computer with appropriate software, web access, digital camera, color laser printer, photographs, public service announcements, programs, historical and descriptive literature, and biographical information.

STANDARD: Ensuring the press package contains all current required information and is prepared with 100% accuracy.

PERFORMANCE STEPS:
1. Compile current material.
2. Organize all materials into a structured format.

REFERENCES:
1. MCO P5000.18_ Marine Corps Band Manual
2. SECNAVINST 5720.44_ Public Affairs Policy and Regulations
3. StratCom - Strategic Communication Plan PCN 50100654400, dated July 2007

5524-CREL-2023: Maintain websites

EVALUATION-CODED: NO   **SUSTAINMENT INTERVAL:** 12 months

BILLETS: Webmaster

GRADES: CPL, SGT, SSGT, GYSGT

INITIAL TRAINING SETTING: MOJT

CONDITION: Given a computer with access to an official DoD server, appropriate software, appropriate permissions, and updated Band information.

STANDARD: Ensuring data is current and 100% accurate on both local and Headquarters Marine Corps websites.

PERFORMANCE STEPS:
1. Acquire DoD server.
2. Obtain all pertinent authorized information.
3. Verify edited site information and links.

REFERENCES:
1. MCO 5720.76 Standardization of Publicly Accessible Web Pages
2. SECNAVINST 5720.44_ Public Affairs Policy and Regulations
3. StratCom - Strategic Communication Plan PCN 50100654400, dated July 2007
4. www.marines.mil/community

5524-FDRL-2030: Lead field drill

EVALUATION-CODED: NO   **SUSTAINMENT INTERVAL:** 12 months

BILLETS: Musician

GRADES: SSGT, GYSGT

INITIAL TRAINING SETTING: MOJT

CONDITION: Given a mace, a fully equipped band, and marching area.

STANDARD: Ensuring maneuver is performed in accordance with the sequence of events and at a proper marching tempo to the Occupational Field standard.

PERFORMANCE STEPS:
1. Brief the sequence of events to the Band.
2. Dictate maneuver using verbal commands or mace signals, as appropriate.
3. Correct music and drill, as appropriate.
4. Execute sequence of events.
5. Program appropriate music.

REFERENCES:
1. MCO P5000.18_ Marine Corps Band Manual
2. MCO P5060.20_ Marine Corps Drill and Ceremonies Manual
3. U.S. Navy Regulations w/Ch 1 Chapter 12 - Flags, Pennants, Honors, Ceremonies, and Customs

---

5524-PERF-2050: Lead Ceremonial Band

EVALUATION-CODED: NO   **SUSTAINMENT INTERVAL:** 12 months

BILLETS: Musician

GRADES: SSGT, GYSGT

INITIAL TRAINING SETTING: MOJT

CONDITION: Given a baton, a fully equipped band, and a performance venue.

STANDARD: Ensuring music is performed in accordance with the prescribed sequence of events and to the Occupational Field standard.

PERFORMANCE STEPS:
1. Brief the sequence of events to the Band.

2. Conduct Band using proper baton techniques.
3. Correct music in rehearsal, as appropriate.
4. Execute sequence of events.
5. Program appropriate music.

REFERENCES:
1. MCO P5000.18_ Marine Corps Band Manual
2. MCO P5060.20__ Marine Corps Drill and Ceremonies Manual
3. U.S. Navy Regulations Chapter 12 -Flags, Pennants, Honors, Ceremonies, and Customs

---

5524-PERF-2051: Write concert narration

EVALUATION-CODED: NO   **SUSTAINMENT INTERVAL:** 12 months

BILLETS: Musician

GRADES: CPL, SGT, SSGT, GYSGT

INITIAL TRAINING SETTING: MOJT

CONDITION: When assigned and given a computer, reference material, and the list of programmed music.

STANDARD: Ensuring correct grammar, accuracy of information, and pertinence to concert venue.

PERFORMANCE STEPS:
1. Obtain concert program.
2. Coordinate with unit commander to capture intent.
3. Draft concert notes.
4. Submit for approval.

REFERENCE:
1. MCO P5000.18_ Marine Corps Band Manual

5524-PERF-2052: Narrate concert

EVALUATION-CODED: NO   **SUSTAINMENT INTERVAL:** 12 months

BILLETS: Musician

GRADES: LCPL, CPL, SGT, SSGT, GYSGT, MSGT, MGYSGT

INITIAL TRAINING SETTING: MOJT

CONDITION: When assigned, given prepared concert notes, and preparation time with the Band.

STANDARD: In accordance with concert notes to ensure an uninterrupted transition between musical selections.

PERFORMANCE STEPS:
1. Review concert notes.
2. Coordinate last minute details with conductor.
3. Establish rapport with audience.
4. Employ intermittent eye contact with audience and Band.
5. Improvise narration, as required.
6. Conclude narration.

REFERENCE:
1. MCO P5000.18_ Marine Corps Band Manual

5524-PERF-2053: Improvise from lead sheet/chord changes

EVALUATION-CODED: NO   **SUSTAINMENT INTERVAL:** 12 months

BILLETS: Musician

GRADES: CPL, SGT, SSGT, GYSGT

INITIAL TRAINING SETTING: MOJT

CONDITION: When required, given an assembled instrument, and a lead sheet.

STANDARD: To create a stylistically appropriate musical solo within proper chord structure.

PERFORMANCE STEPS:
1. Study lead sheet with chord changes.
2. Perform a melody consistent with the style of the composition.

REFERENCES:
1. AEBERSOLD, JAMEY. ALBUMS AND TEXT; Publisher: Charles Colin Music Publications
2. MCO P5000.18_ Marine Corps Band Manual

5524-PERF-2054: Lead small ensemble performance

EVALUATION-CODED: NO   **SUSTAINMENT INTERVAL:** 12 months

BILLETS: Musician

GRADES: CPL, SGT, SSGT, GYSGT

INITIAL TRAINING SETTING: MOJT

DESCRIPTION: Required small ensembles are defined in the MCO P5000.18_.

CONDITION: Given an equipped ensemble and proper music.

STANDARD: Ensuring notes, rhythm, and style are produced with 100% accuracy.

PERFORMANCE STEPS:
1. Brief the sequence of events to the ensemble.
2. Correct music in rehearsal as appropriate.
3. Execute sequence of events.
4. Program appropriate music.

REFERENCE:
1. MCO P5000.18_ Marine Corps Band Manual

5524-PERF-2055: Assemble audio/visual equipment

EVALUATION-CODED: NO   **SUSTAINMENT INTERVAL:** 12 months

BILLETS: Musician

GRADES: PVT, PFC, LCPL, CPL, SGT, SSGT, GYSGT

INITIAL TRAINING SETTING: MOJT

CONDITION: When assigned to sound crew, given audio/visual equipment, and a venue.

STANDARD: Ensuring 100% operability and proper placement of equipment.

PERFORMANCE STEPS:
1. Receive plan from unit leader
2. Properly assemble equipment.
3. Properly place equipment according to plan.
4. Connect equipment.
5. Test equipment operability.

REFERENCES:
1. DAVIS & JONES YAMAHA SOUND REINFORCEMENT HANDBOOK
2. MCO P5000.18_ Marine Corps Band Manual
3. STARK, S. H. LIVE SOUND REINFORCEMENT

5524-PERF-2056: Operate audio/visual equipment

EVALUATION-CODED: NO   **SUSTAINMENT INTERVAL:** 12 months

BILLETS: Sound Chief

GRADES: CPL, SGT, SSGT, GYSGT

INITIAL TRAINING SETTING: FORMAL

CONDITION: Given operable audio/visual and recording equipment, a performing ensemble, sound crew, and a venue.

STANDARD: To ensure sound reinforcement and audio/visual recordings per industry standard.

PERFORMANCE STEPS:
1. Set-up equipment.
2. Conduct sound check.
3. Execute performance.
4. Produce audio/visual product.

REFERENCES:
1. DAVIS & JONES YAMAHA SOUND REINFORCEMENT HANDBOOK
2. FABER, S. RECORDING HANDBOOK
3. STARK, S. H. LIVE SOUND REINFORCEMENT

5524-PERF-2057: Perform vocal music

EVALUATION-CODED: NO   **SUSTAINMENT INTERVAL:** 12 months

BILLETS: Musician

GRADES: PFC, LCPL, CPL, SGT, SSGT, GYSGT

INITIAL TRAINING SETTING: FORMAL

DESCRIPTION: Prior to assignment as a vocalist, Primary MOS proficiency must be commensurate with grade.

CONDITION: When assigned as vocalist, of a performing ensemble, given appropriate music, and a conductor or ensemble leader.

STANDARD: Ensure notes, tone quality, rhythm, style, musicality and showmanship are accurately produced to industry standard.

PERFORMANCE STEPS:
1. Perform the music, following the conductor's direction.
2. Make individual adjustments, as necessary, to provide proper balance within the ensemble.

REFERENCE:
1.   MCO P5000.18_ Marine Corps Band Manual

5524-REHL-2060: Lead section rehearsal

EVALUATION-CODED: NO   **SUSTAINMENT INTERVAL:** 6 months

BILLETS: Musician

GRADES: SGT, SSGT, GYSGT

INITIAL TRAINING SETTING: MOJT

CONDITION: Given rehearsal objectives, a group of equipped instrumentalists, appropriate rehearsal space, music, and auxiliary equipment.

STANDARD: To detect and correct errors and provide performance guidance through gestures and verbal instruction, within the scheduled rehearsal time to the occupational field standard.

PERFORMANCE STEPS:
1. Study scores for designated music.
2. Convey rehearsal objectives.
3. Ensure section is properly tuned.
4. Provide guidance for any identified errors.
5. Provide verbal feedback for next rehearsal.

REFERENCE:
1. MCO P5000.18_ Marine Corps Band Manual

5524-SUPT-2070: Supervise Library Section

EVALUATION-CODED: NO   **SUSTAINMENT INTERVAL**: 6 months

BILLETS: Musician, Band Library Chief

GRADES: SSGT, GYSGT

INITIAL TRAINING SETTING: MOJT

CONDITION: Given assigned band personnel, required library material, sheet music, music texts, reference materials, and music publications.

STANDARD: To ensure that all required music materials are on hand, current, properly accounted for and maintained in an organized manner.

PERFORMANCE STEPS:
1. Train assigned personnel to execute all required library functions.
2. Verify that all stored library materials/equipment are well maintained.
3. Verify that library inventory is complete and accurate.
4. Request purchase of required library materials/equipment, as needed.
5. Ensure accuracy of performance log.

REFERENCES:
1. BYRNE, FRANK PRACTICAL GUIDE TO THE MUSIC LIBRARY: ITS FUNCTION, ORGANIZATION AND MAINTENANCE; Publisher: Ludwig Music Company (December 1987)
2. MCO P5000.18_ Marine Corps Band Manual
3. PUBLIC LAW 94-553 Federal Copyright Act, Title 17 of U. S. Code
4. U. S. Navy Regulations w/Ch 1 Chapter 12 - Flags, Pennants, Honors, Ceremonies, and Customs

---

5524-SUPT-2071: Supervise Supply Section

EVALUATION-CODED: NO   **SUSTAINMENT INTERVAL**: 12 months

BILLETS: Supply Chief

GRADES: SSGT, GYSGT

INITIAL TRAINING SETTING: MOJT

CONDITION: Given appropriate catalogues, forms, computer, unit supply database, climate controlled secure storage facility, administrative supplies, and procurement requirements.

STANDARD: To procure, issue, and account for Band equipment and instruments with 100% accuracy.

PERFORMANCE STEPS:
1. Update unit records and Consolidated Memorandum Receipt as required.
2 Maintain custody cards.
3. Conduct inventory of all equipment on unit TO&E.
4. Create list of discrepancies.
5. Create reconciliation report.
6. Update inventory records.
7. Maintain disposal procedures.

REFERENCES:
1. MCO 4400.163 DoD Supply Management Reference Book
2. MCO P4200.15 Marine Corps Purchasing Procedures Manual
3. MCO P4400.150_ W/ERRATUM CH 1-2 Consumer Level Policy Manual
4. MCO P5000.18_ Marine Corps Band Manual

5524-SUPT-2072: Inventory Band equipment

EVALUATION-CODED: NO   SUSTAINMENT INTERVAL: 12 months

BILLETS: Supply Clerk

GRADES: CPL, SGT, SSGT

INITIAL TRAINING SETTING: MOJT

CONDITION: Given a current Consolidated Memorandum of Receipt (CMR).

STANDARD: In performance step sequence, reconcile on-hand items with the CMR accurately notating any discrepancies.

PERFORMANCE STEPS:
1. Conduct inventory.
2. Submit discrepancy report.
3. Reconcile discrepancy report.
4. Update records.

REFERENCES:
1. MCO 4400.163 DoD Supply Management Reference Book
2. MCO P5000.18_ Marine Corps Band Manual

5524-SUPT-2073: Supervise Administrative Section

EVALUATION-CODED: NO   **SUSTAINMENT INTERVAL**: 12 months

BILLETS: Admin Chief

GRADES: SSGT, GYSGT

INITIAL TRAINING SETTING: MOJT

CONDITION: Given an Administrative Section, forms, computers, a fax, a scanner, a copy machine, unit personnel database, an appropriate office space, and administrative supplies and equipment.

STANDARD: Ensuring all administrative function are completed in an efficient and timely manner with 100% accuracy.

PERFORMANCE STEPS:
1. Ensure submission of command chronology.
2. Oversee correspondence production.
3. Oversee correspondence filing.
4. Ensure timely roster updates.
5. Process performance requests.
6. Oversee maintenance of personnel records.
7. Oversee publication of planning documents.

REFERENCES:
1. MCO P5000.18_ Marine Corps Band Manual
2. SECNAVINST 5216.5D w/Ch 1-2 Department of the Navy (DON) correspondence Manual
3. SECNAVINST M-5210.2 Standard Subject Identification Codes
4. SECNAVINST M-5210.1 Department of the Navy (DON) Records Management Program
5. SECNAVINST 5212.5 Navy and Marine Corps Records Disposal Manual
6. MCO 5210.11_ Marine Corps Records Management

5524-SUPT-2074: Supervise Training Section

EVALUATION-CODED: NO   **SUSTAINMENT INTERVAL**: 12 months

BILLETS: Training Chief

GRADES: SSGT, GYSGT

INITIAL TRAINING SETTING: MOJT

CONDITION: Given a Training Section, forms, a computer, a unit personnel database, appropriate office space, training equipment, and administrative supplies and equipment.

STANDARD: Ensuring all training functions are completed in an efficient and timely manner with 100% accuracy and safety.

PERFORMANCE STEPS:
1. Coordinate with S-3 for training events.
2. Develop unit training schedule.
3. Oversee conduct of unit training.
4. Oversee production of training rosters.
5. Ensure timely roster updates.
6. Coordinate Professional Military Education (PME).
7. Oversee maintenance of training records.

REFERENCES:
1. MCO P5000.18_ Marine Corps Band Manual
2. MCO 1553.3A Unit Training Management
3. MCO P6100.13 Marine Corps Physical Fitness Program
4. MCO 6110.3 Marine Corps Body Composition and Military Appearance Program
5. MCO 1500.54A Marine Corps Martial Arts Program
6. MCO 1553.4B Profession Military Education

5524-SUPT-2075: Supervise Loading Section

EVALUATION-CODED: NO   **SUSTAINMENT INTERVAL:** 12 months

BILLETS: Loading Chief

GRADES: SGT, SSGT

INITIAL TRAINING SETTING: MOJT

CONDITION: Given a mode of transportation and equipment and loading crew.

STANDARD: Ensure all required equipment is efficiently loaded in a safe manner with 100% accountability.

PERFORMANCE STEPS:
1. Liaise with unit leader.
2. Create manifest.
3. Oversee loading/unloading of equipment.

REFERENCES:
1. MCO P5000.18_ Marine Corps Band Manual
2. MCO 5100.8 Marine Corps Occupational Safety and Health Policy Order
3. MCO 3500.27 Operational Risk Management

5524-SUPT-2076: Supervise Transportation Section

EVALUATION-CODED: NO   **SUSTAINMENT INTERVAL:** 12 months

BILLETS: Transportation Chief

GRADES: SGT, SSGT, GYSGT

INITIAL TRAINING SETTING: MOJT

CONDITION: Given a transportation requirement, Transportation Section, forms, a computer, a commitment calendar, appropriate office space, and administrative supplies and equipment.

STANDARD: To meet transportation requirements to 100% accuracy without incident.

PERFORMANCE STEPS:
1. Ensure timely submissions of all transportation requests.
2. Ensure unit has adequate number of trained drivers, as required.
3. Develop a transportation plan.
4. Schedule vehicle maintenance, as required.

REFERENCE:
1. MCO P5000.18_ Marine Corps Band Manual

5524-SUPT-2077: Supervise DTS Section

EVALUATION-CODED: NO   **SUSTAINMENT INTERVAL**: 12 months

BILLETS: DTS Chief

GRADES: SGT, SSGT, GYSGT

INITIAL TRAINING SETTING: Distance Learning

CONDITION: Given a computer, roster of personnel, and a TAD requirement.

STANDARD: To meet unit DTS requirements to 100% accuracy.

PERFORMANCE STEPS:
1. Acquire line of accounting as required.
2. Oversee generation of orders.
3. Assist in liquidation of voucher.

REFERENCE:
DTS Manual Version 4.4.28, updated 25 Aug 2010

9005. 2500-LEVEL EVENTS

<u>5524-ADMN-2501</u>: Supervise Band Intermediate Leadership

<u>EVALUATION-CODED</u>: NO   <u>SUSTAINMENT INTERVAL</u>: 12 months

<u>BILLETS</u>: Bandmaster

<u>GRADES</u>: MSGT, MGYSGT

<u>INITIAL TRAINING SETTING</u>: FORMAL

<u>DESCRIPTION</u>: Band Intermediate Leadership includes Drum Major, Enlisted Conductor, Small Ensemble Leader, Platoon Sergeant, and Training Chief.

<u>CONDITION</u>: Given Band personnel.

<u>STANDARD</u>: To ensure all assigned areas remain 100% mission capable.

<u>PERFORMANCE STEPS</u>:
1. Inspect Drum Major responsibilities.
2. Inspect Enlisted Conductor responsibilities.
3. Inspect Small Ensemble Leader responsibilities.
4. Inspect Platoon Sergeant responsibilities.
5. Inspect Training Chief responsibilities.
6. Mentor assigned personnel.

<u>REFERENCE</u>:
1. MCO P5000.18_ Marine Corps Band Manual

<u>5524-AUDN-2510</u>: Audition personnel

<u>EVALUATION-CODED</u>: NO   <u>SUSTAINMENT INTERVAL</u>: 6 months

<u>BILLETS</u>: Bandmaster

<u>GRADES</u>: MSGT, MGYSGT

<u>INITIAL TRAINING SETTING</u>: FORMAL

<u>CONDITION</u>: Given an instrumentalist with instrument, music stand, audition book, administrative materials, copy of auditionee's solo, metronome, and designated location.

<u>STANDARD</u>: In performance step sequence, to ascertain technical proficiency and ensuring 98% accuracy and consistency with the Audition Standards Manual.

<u>PERFORMANCE STEPS</u>:
1. Grade prepared material.
2. Grade performance of rudiments or scales.
3. Grade performance of sight reading material.

4. Average numerical score for all criteria.
5. Evaluate memorized music as required.

REFERENCES:
1. MCO P5000.18_ Marine Corps Band Manual
2. MUSCOLINST 1300.1 Audition Standards Manual

5524-AUDN-2511: Audition prospective applicant

EVALUATION-CODED: NO   **SUSTAINMENT INTERVAL:** 6 months

BILLETS: Bandmaster

GRADES: MSGT, MGYSGT

INITIAL TRAINING SETTING: FORMAL

CONDITION: Given a prospective Marine musician applicant with instrument, music stand, audition book, administrative materials, an audition form, a MEOP screening form, copy of auditionee's solo, metronome, designated location, and in a garrison environment.

STANDARD: In performance step sequence, to ascertain technical proficiency and ensuring 98% accuracy and consistency with the Audition Standards Manual.

PERFORMANCE STEPS:
1. Screen prospective applicant.
2. Establish rapport with applicant.
3. Establish proper audition environment.
4. Determine if prepared solo meets required difficulty level.
5. Review auditions process with applicant.
6. Provide warm-up opportunity, if required.
7. Evaluate auditionee's competency by observing musical criteria demonstrated.
8. Describe each criterion observed in descriptive adjectives criteria form.
9. Record numerical score for each criterion that most accurately corresponds to descriptive adjective.
10. Average numerical score for all criteria.
11. Record final average in appropriate block on audition form.
12. Counsel auditionee on final results.
13. File copy of audition form.
14. Forward results, as required.

REFERENCES:
1. MCO P5000.18_ Marine Corps Band Manual
2. MUSCOLINST 1300.1 Audition Standards Manual
3. MCO 1200.17_ Military Occupational Specialties Manual

5524-CREL-2520: Deliver Marine Corps Band marketing presentation

EVALUATION-CODED: NO   **SUSTAINMENT INTERVAL:** 12 months

BILLETS: Bandmaster

GRADES: MSGT, MGYSGT

INITIAL TRAINING SETTING: FORMAL

CONDITION: Given a targeted audience, current Band information, and computer with presentation software.

STANDARD: To clearly and concisely address current leadership and performance opportunities within Marine Corps Bands.

PERFORMANCE STEPS:
1. Schedule presentation.
2. Gather demographic information on civilian musical unit.
3. Prepare presentation outline.
4. Rehearse presentation outline.
5. Deliver presentation.
6. Answer questions.
7. Provide feedback to Marine Corps Recruiting Command.

REFERENCES:
1. MCO 1130.53P w/CH 1 Enlistment Incentive Programs
2. MCO 5726.15 Marine Corps Band Support of Community Relations
3. MCO P5000.18_ Marine Corps Band Manual
4. MCRC VOLUME 3-Guidebook for Recruiting Station Operations

5524-PLAN-2560: Develop annual operational plan

EVALUATION-CODED: NO   **SUSTAINMENT INTERVAL**: 12 months

BILLETS: Bandmaster

GRADES: MSGT, MGYSGT

INITIAL TRAINING SETTING: MOJT

CONDITION: Given previous year's command chronology, projected military requirements, recruiting command support, community relations events, and unit sustainment training requirements.

STANDARD: Ensuring all national and local support requirements and periods of non-availability are reflected.

PERFORMANCE STEPS:
1. Prioritize requirements.
2. Determine operational tempo.
3. Identify projected periods of non-availability for training evolutions.
4. Schedule annual training events.
5. Identify projected periods for supporting national community relations events.
6. Identify projected periods of non-availability for leave.
7. Reconcile conflicts.

8. Forward to Band Officer for approval.
9. Publish plan.

REFERENCES:
1. MCO 5726.15 Marine Corps Band Support of Community Relations
2. MCO P5000.18B Marine Corps Band Manual
3. StratCom - Strategic Communication Plan PCN 50100654400, dtd July 2007

5524-PLAN-2561: Develop Band schedule

EVALUATION-CODED: NO   **SUSTAINMENT INTERVAL:** 12 months

BILLETS: Bandmaster

GRADES: MSGT, MGYSGT

INITIAL TRAINING SETTING: MOJT

CONDITION: Given a list of approved commitments, training requirements, personnel, and equipment.

STANDARD: To ensure all training requirements are met and the unit remains mission capable for all approved commitments.

PERFORMANCE STEPS:
1. Obtain ensemble leaders' rehearsal requirements.
2. Obtain logistical requirements.
3. Review training requirements.
4. Prioritize requirements.
5. Review Band commitment schedule.
6. Resolve identified conflicts.
7. Forward to Band Officer for approval.
8. Publish schedule.

REFERENCE:
1. MCO P5000.18_ Marine Corps Band Manual

5524-PLAN-2562: Evaluate commitment requests

EVALUATION-CODED: NO   **SUSTAINMENT INTERVAL:** 12 months

BILLETS: Bandmaster

GRADES: MSGT, MGYSGT

INITIAL TRAINING SETTING: MOJT

CONDITION: Given a commitment request, annual operation plan, Band schedule, and funding requirements.

STANDARD: To accurately determine feasibility of support.

PERFORMANCE STEPS:
1. Review Band schedule.
2. Contact sponsor for additional information.
3. Evaluate legality of commitment.
4. Determine musical support requirements.
5. Determine logistical support requirements.
6. Verify availability of appropriate ensemble for request.
7. Recommend approval or disapproval.
8. Forward to Band Officer.

REFERENCES:
1. MCO 5726.15 Marine Corps Band Support of Community Relations
2. MCO P5000.18_ Marine Corps Band Manual
3. SECNAVINST 5720.44B Public Affairs Policy and Regulations
4. Local Standard Operating Procedures

MUSIC T&R MANUAL

APPENDIX A

ACRONYMS AND ABBREVIATIONS

AA . . . . .administrative action
CBT. . . . . .computer based training
CMC . . . . .Commandant of the Marine Corps
CG. . . . . .commanding general
CO . . . . commanding officer
COA. . . . . course of action
COMMARFOR . . . . Commander, Marine Corps Forces
COMMARFORLANT . . . . Commander, Marine Corps Forces, Atlantic
COMMARFORPAC . . . . Commander, Marine Corps Forces, Pacific
CMR. . . . . Consolidated Memorandum of Receipt
Cpl. . . . . Corporal
CONPLAN. . . . . Contingency Plan
CONUS . . . . Continental United States
CRP. . . . . .combat readiness percentage
CTS. . . . . .collective training standards
CWO2. . . . . Chief Warrant Officer-2
CWO3. . . . . Chief Warrant Officer-3
CWO4. . . . . Chief Warrant Officer-4
CWO5. . . . . Chief Warrant Officer-5
CY. . . . . calendar year
DL. . . . . distance learning
DoD . . . . Department of Defense
DoDD . . . . Department of Defense Directive
DoDI . . . . Department of Defense Instruction
DON . . . . Department of the Navy
DRMO. . . . . Defense Reutilization Management Office
DRRS. . . . . .Defense Readiness Reporting System
E-Coded. . . . . Evaluation-Coded
FMF . . . . Fleet Marine Force
FMFM . . . . Fleet Marine Force Manual
FY . . . . .fiscal year
GTCCP . . . . Government Travel Charge Card Program
GYSGT. . . . . Gunnery Sergeant
HAZMAT. . . . . .hazardous material
HMIS. .Hazardous Material Information Sheet
HPD. . . . . .hearing protection device
HQMC . . . . Headquarters, Marine Corps
IMI. . . . . individual multimedia instruction
ITS. . . . . .individual training standards
JCS . . . . Joint Chiefs of Staff
JFTR . . . . Joint Federal Travel Regulations
JP. . . . . Joint Publication
LCPL. . . . . .Lance Corporal
MACOM . . . . major command
MAGTF . . . . Marine Air-Ground Task Force
MARDIV . . . . Marine Division
MARFOR . . . . Marine Corps Forces

```
MCB . . . . . . . . . . . . . . . . . . . . . . . . . . . . Marine Corps Base
MCBUL. . . . . . . . . . . . . . . . . . . . . . . . . .Marine Corps Bulletin
MCCRES. . . . . . . . . . . . . .Marine Corps Readiness and Evaluation System
MCCS . . . . . . . . . . . . . . . . . . . . . . . Marine Corps Common Skills
MCI. . . . . . . . . . . . . . . . . . . . . . . . . Marine Corps Institute
MCO . . . . . . . . . . . . . . . . . . . . . . . . . . . Marine Corps Order
MCRC. . . . . . . . . . . . . . . . . . . . . Marine Corps Recruiting Command
MCTL. . . . . . . . . . . . . . . . . . . . . . . .Marine Corps Task List
MCRP. . . . . . . . . . . . . . . . . . .Marine Corps Reference Publication
MCWST. . . . . . . . . . . . . . . . . . Marine Corps Water Survival Training
MEF . . . . . . . . . . . . . . . . . . . . . . . Marine Expeditionary Force
MET. . . . . . . . . . . . . . . . . . . . . . . . . . Mission Essential Task
METL. . . . . . . . . . . . . . . . . . . . . . . Mission Essential Task List
MEU . . . . . . . . . . . . . . . . . . . . . . . . Marine Expeditionary Unit
MGYSGT. . . . . . . . . . . . . . . . . . . . . . Master Gunnery Sergeant
MLSR. . . . . . . . . . . . . . . . . . . . .missing, lost, stolen or recovered
MOJT . . . . . . . . . . . . . . . . . . . . . managed on the job training
MOS. . . . . . . . . . . . . . . . . . . . . .Military Occupational Specialty
MSC . . . . . . . . . . . . . . . . . . . . . . . . major subordinate command
MSDS. . . . . . . . . . . . . . . . . . . . . . .Material Safety Data Sheet
MSGT. . . . . . . . . . . . . . . . . . . . . . . . . . . . Master Sergeant
MSE . . . . . . . . . . . . . . . . . . . . . . . . major subordinate element
MURE. . . . . . . . . . . . . . . . . . . . . . .Musical Unit Resources Exhibit
MUSC. . . . . . . . . . . . . . . . . . . . . . . . . . . . . . . . . . Music
MUSCOLINST. . . . . . . . . . . . . . . . . . . . . . . . Music Instruction
MWR . . . . . . . . . . . . . . . . . . . . . . morale, welfare and recreation
NATO. . . . . . . . . . . . . . . . . . . . .North Atlantic Treaty Organization
NAVEDTRA. . . . . . . . . . . . . . . . . . .Naval Education Training Command
NAVMC . . . . . . . . . . . . . . . . . . . . . . . . . Navy and Marine Corps
NBC. . . . . . . . . . . . . . . . . . . . . . nuclear, biological and chemical
NBCD. . . . . . . . . . . . . . Nuclear, Biological, and Chemical Defense
OccFld . . . . . . . . . . . . . . . . . . . . . . . . . . occupational field
OCONUS . . . . . . . . . . . . . . . . . . outside the Continental United States
OPLAN. . . . . . . . . . . . . . . . . . . . . . . . . . . .Operations Plan
OPNAVINST . . . . . . . .Office of the Chief of Naval Operations Instruction
OR. . . . . . . . . . . . . . . . . . . . . . . . . . operational readiness
ORM. . . . . . . . . . . . . . . . . . . . . . . .Operational Risk Management
PFC. . . . . . . . . . . . . . . . . . . . . . . . . .Private First Class
POD. . . . . . . . . . . . . . . . . . . . . . . . . . .Plan of the Day
PPE. . . . . . . . . . . . . . . . . . . . . . .Personal Protective Equipment
PRP. . . . . . . . . . . . . . . . . . . . . . . . . .Periodic Replacement Plan
PVT. . . . . . . . . . . . . . . . . . . . . . . . . . . . . . . . . .Private
S-1. . . . . . . . . . . . . . . . . . . . .manpower or personnel staff officer
S-2. . . . . . . . . . . . . . . . . . . . . . . . intelligence staff officer
S-3. . . . . . . . . . . . . . . . . . . . . . . . . operations staff officer
SAT. . . . . . . . . . . . . . . . . . . . . . . Systems Approach to Training
SECNAVINST . . . . . . . . . . . . . . . . . .Secretary of the Navy instruction
SGT. . . . . . . . . . . . . . . . . . . . . . . . . . . . . . . . . Sergeant
SME. . . . . . . . . . . . . . . . . . . . . . . . . . . .subject matter expert
SNCO. . . . . . . . . . . . . . . . . . . . . . .Staff Non-Commissioned Officer
SSGT. . . . . . . . . . . . . . . . . . . . . . . . . . . . .Staff Sergeant
TAD . . . . . . . . . . . . . . . . . . . . . . . . . temporary additional duty
TECOM. . . . . . . . . . . . . . . . . . . . . . Training and Education Command
T/E . . . . . . . . . . . . . . . . . . . . . . . . . . . . table of equipment
T/O . . . . . . . . . . . . . . . . . . . . . . . . . . . table of organization
```

T&R. . . . . Training and Readiness
U.S. . . . . .United States
UST. . . . . .Unit Sustainment Training
UTM. . . . . unit training management
WO1. . . . . Warrant Officer-1

APPENDIX B

TERMS AND DEFINITIONS

Terms in this glossary are subject to change as applicable orders and directives are revised. Terms established by Marine Corps orders or directives take precedence after definitions found in Joint Pub (JP) 1-02, DoD Dictionary of Military and Associated Terms.

A

After Action Review (AAR). A professional discussion of training events conducted after all training to promote learning among training participants. The formality and scope increase with the command level and size of the training evolution. For longer exercises, they should be planned for at predetermined times during an exercise. The results of the AAR shall be recorded on an after action report and forwarded to higher headquarters. The commander and higher headquarters use the results of an AAR to reallocate resources, reprioritize their training plan, and plan for future training.

C

Chaining. A process that enables unit leaders to effectively identify subordinate collective events and individual events that support a specific collective event. For example, collective training events at the 4000-level are directly supported by collective events at the 3000-level. Utilizing the building block approach to progressive training, these collective events are further supported by individual training events at the 1000 and 2000-levels. When a higher-level event by its nature requires the completion of lower level events, they are "chained"; Sustainment credit is given for all lower level events chained to a higher event.

D

Deception. Those measures designed to mislead the enemy by manipulation, distortion, or falsification of evidence to induce the enemy to react in a manner prejudicial to the enemy's interests. (JP 1-02)

E

E-Coded Event. An "E-Coded" event is a collective T&R event that is a noted indicator of capability or, a noted Collective skill that contributes to the unit's ability to perform the supported MET. As such, only "E-Coded" events are assigned a CRP value and used to calculate a unit's CRP.

I

Individual Readiness. The individual training readiness of each Marine is measured by the number of individual events required and completed for the rank or billet currently held.

M

Marine Corps Combat Readiness and Evaluation System (MCCRES). An evaluation system designed to provide commanders with a comprehensive set of mission performance standards from which training programs can be developed; and through which the efficiency and effectiveness of training can be evaluated. The Ground T&R Program will eventually replace MCCRES.

O

Operational Readiness (OR). (DoD or NATO) OR is the capability of a unit/formation, ship, weapon system, or equipment to perform the missions or functions for which it is organized or designed. May be used in a general sense or to express a level or degree of readiness.

P

Performance Step. Performance steps are included in the components of an Individual T&R Event. They are the major procedures (i.e., actions) a Marine unit must accomplish to perform an individual event to standard. They describe the procedure the task performer must take to perform the task under operational conditions and provide sufficient information for a task performer to perform the procedure (may necessitate identification of supporting steps, procedures, or actions in outline form). Performance steps follow a logical progression and should be followed sequentially, unless otherwise stated. Normally, performance steps are listed only for 1000-level individual events (those that are taught in the entry-level MOS school). Listing performance steps is optional if the steps are already specified in a published reference.

R

Readiness. (DoD) Readiness is the ability of U.S. military forces to fight and meet the demands of the national military strategy. Readiness is the synthesis of two distinct but interrelated levels: Unit readiness - the ability to provide capabilities required by combatant commanders to execute assigned missions. This is derived from the ability of each unit to deliver the outputs for which it was designed. And Joint readiness - the combatant commander's ability to integrate and synchronize ready combat and support forces to execute assigned missions.

S

Section Skill Tasks. Section skills are those competencies directly related to unit functioning. They are group rather than individual in nature, and require participation by a section (S-1, S-2, S-3, etc).

T

Training Task. This describes a direct training activity that pertains to an individual Marine. A task is composed of three major components: a description of what is to be done, a condition, and a standard.

U

Unit CRP. Unit CRP is a percentage of the E-coded collective events that support the unit METL accomplished by the unit. Unit CRP is the average of all MET CRP.

W

Waived Event. An event that is waived by a commanding officer when in his or her judgment, previous experience or related performance satisfies the requirement of a particular event.

APPENDIX C

REFERENCES

PUBLICATION ID	TITLE
A	
MCO P1000.6G	Assignment, Classification and Travel Systems Manual (ACTS MANUAL)
	AEBERSOLD, JAMEY; ALBUMS AND TEXT; Publisher: Charles Colin Music Publications
MUSCOLINST 1300.1	Audition Standards Manual
B	
	Bassoon Reed Making: An Illustrated Method, Christopher Wait, 3008
	Bassoon Reed Making, 3rd Edition, Mark Popkin and Loren Glickman, 2007
	BECKWITH, GENE E.; HUTH, JOHN; BAND INSTRUMENT REPAIR MANUAL; Publisher: Minnesota SE Technical College (2001)
	BRAND, ERICK D.; BAND INSTRUMENT REPAIRING MANUAL; Ferree's Tools Inc. (1993)
	BYRNE, FRANK; PRACTICAL GUIDE TO THE MUSIC LIBRARY: ITS FUNCTION, ORGANIZATION AND MAINTENANCE; Publisher: Ludwig Music Company (December 1987)
C	
U. S. Navy Regulations, 1990, w/Ch 1	Chapter 12 - Flags, Pennants, Honors, Ceremonies and Customs
MCO P4400.150E W/ERRATUM Ch 1	Consumer Level Policy Manual
D	
	DAVIS & JONES; YAMAHA SOUND REINFORCEMENT HANDBOOK
UFC 4-171-04AN	Department of Defense Design Guide - Band Training Facilities
MCO 4631.11	Department of Defense Policy on the Use of Government Aircraft and Air Travel
MCO 4400.163	Department of Defense Supply Management Reference Book
SECNAVINST 5216.5D w/Ch 1-2	Department of the Navy (DON) Correspondence Manual
SECNAVINST M-5210.1	Department of the Navy (DON) Records Management Program
DTS Manual	DTS Manual Version 4.4.28 updated 25 Aug 2010
E	
MCO 1130.53P w/ Ch 1	Enlisted Incentive Program
MCO P5090.2A	Environmental Compliance and Protection Manual

F	
	FABER, S.; RECORDING HANDBOOK
Public Law 94-553	Federal Copyright Act, Title 17 of the U.S. Code
MCO P7100.8K	Field Budget Guidance Manual
G	
MCO 4600.40A	Government Travel Charge Card Program (GTCCP)
MCRC Volume 3	Guidebook for Recruiting Station Operations
J	
JFTR	NAVSO P-6034 The Joint Federal Travel Regulations (JFTR), Volume 1
K	
	KRAR, S. F.; MACHINE TOOL OPERATIONS; Publisher: McGraw-Hill Inc. (1983)
M	
MCCO 1200.17	Military Occupational Specialties Manual (MOS MANUAL)
OPNAVINST 4631.2D	Management of Department of the Navy (DON) Airlift Assets
MCO P5750.1G w/Ch 1	Manual for the Marine Corps Historical Program
MCO P5000.18B	Marine Corps Band Manual
MCO 5725.15	Marine Corps Band Support of Community Relations
MCO 1500.121A	Marine Corps Common Skills (MCCS) Program
MCO P5060.20	Marine Corps Drill and Ceremonies Manual
MCO P5102.1	Marine Corps Ground Mishap Reporting
MCO 6260.1E	Marine Corps Hearing Conservation Program
MCO P1070.12 w/ Ch 1	Marine Corps Individual Records Administration Manual (IRAM)
MCO 1500.54A	Marine Corps Martial Arts
MCO 5210.11	Marine Corps Records Management
MCO 5100.8	Marine Corps Occupational Safety and Health (OSH) Policy Order
NAVMC DIR 5100.8	Marine Corps Occupational Safety and Health (OSH) Program Manual (MARCOR OSH PROGRAM MANUAL)
	Marine Corps Opportunities Book
MCO P6100.13	Marine Corps Physical Fitness Test and Body Composition Program Manual
MCO P4200.15	Marine Corps Purchasing Procedures Manual
MCO 5100.29A w/Ch 1	Marine Corps Safety Program
N	
MCBUL 5060	National Anthems and Ceremonies
SECNAVINST 5212.5	Navy and Marine Corps Records Disposal Manual
O	
	The Oboe Reed Book, J. Light, 1983
29 CFR 1910.95	Occupational Safety and Health Standards - Occupational

	Noise Exposure
MCO 3500.27	Operational Risk Management
UM 4400-15	Organic Property Control
P	
MCO P1610.7F	Performance Evaluation System (PES)
MCO 1553.4B	Professional Military Education
SECNAVINST 5720.44B	Public Affairs Policy and Regulations
R	
MCO 4340.1A w/Ch 1	Reporting Missing, Lost, Stolen, or Recovered (MLSR) Government Property
S	
StratCom	Strategic Communication Plan, PCN 50100654400, dtd July 2007
SECNAVINST M-5210.2	Standard Subject Identification Codes
MCO 5720.76	Standardization of Publicly Accessible Web Pages
	STARK, S. H.; LIVE SOUND REINFORCEMENT
MCO 4450.12A	Storage and Handling of Hazardous Materials
U	·
MCO 1553.3A	Unit Training Management
W	
	www.marines.mil/community